ROBERT KROESE
DISILLUSIONED

WESTMARCH
PUBLISHING

This is a work of fiction. Any resemblance to actual persons is purely coincidental.

Published by Westmarch Publishing
westmarchpub.com

For Mom.

....

With thanks to:

- All the Kickstarter supporters who made this book possible, with special thanks to: Dan Tabaka, Christopher Turner, Katherine Nall, Cole Kovac, Eric Sybesma, Cara Miller, Andrea Luhman, Taki Soma, Melissa Allison, Matthew J. McCormick, Neva Cheatwood, Daniel Boucher, Sean Simpson, Josh Creed, and Denise and Chad Rogers;

- my editor at Westmarch Publishing, Richard Ellis Preston, Jr.

- and the sharp-eyed and insightful beta readers who made many helpful suggestions for improving this book: Mark Fitzgerald, Mark Thompson, Chris Turner, and Charity VanDeberg.

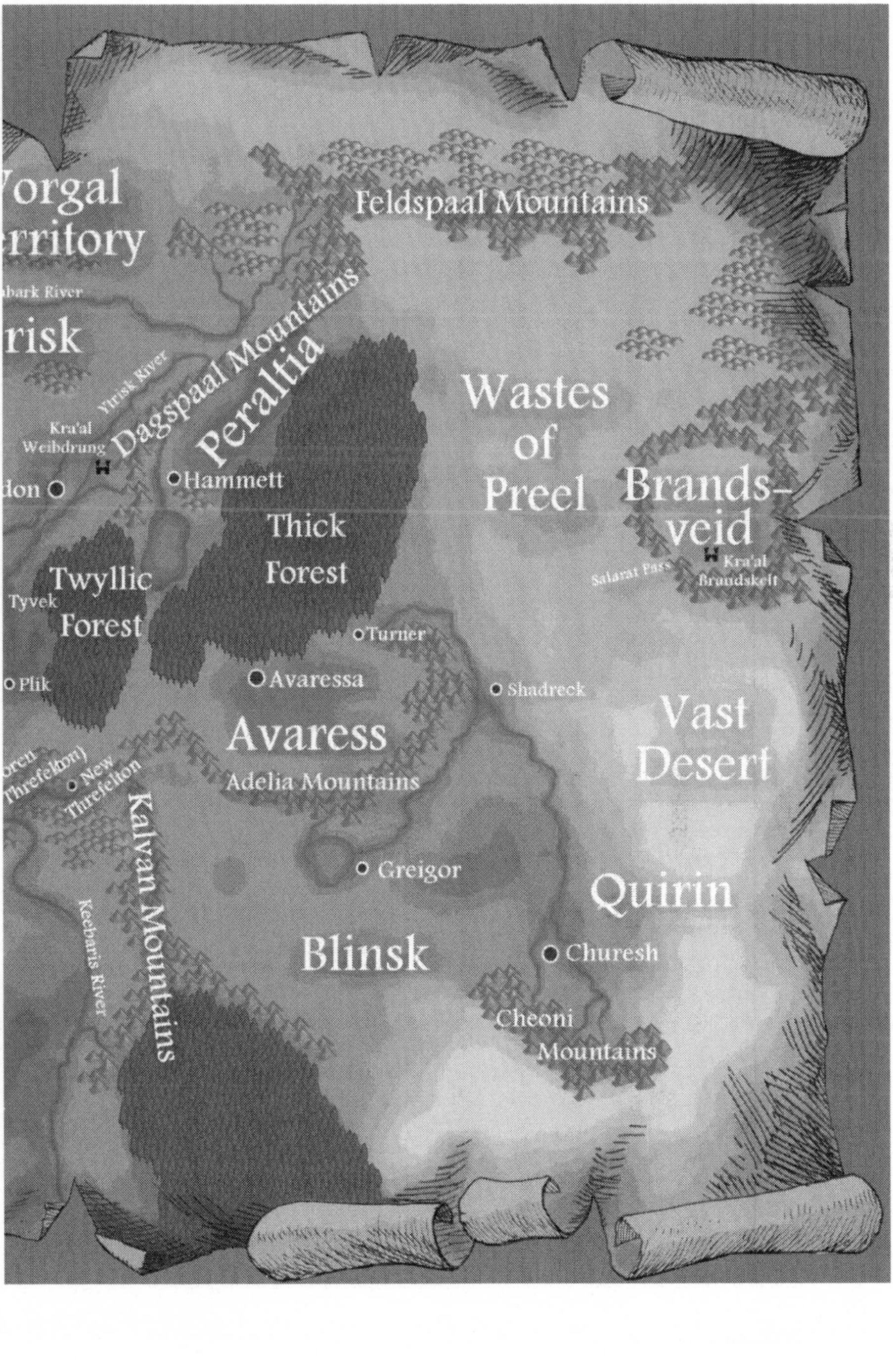

Feldspaal Mountains
Dagspaal Mountains
Peraltia
Yirisk River
Kra'al
Weibdrung
Hammett
Thick
Forest
Wastes
of
Preel
Brands-
veid
Salarat Pass
Kra'al
Brandskelt
Twyllic
Forest
Tyvek
Turner
Plik
Avaressa
Shadreck
Avaress
Vast
Desert
Adelia Mountains
New
Threfelton
Kalvan Mountains
Greigor
Quirin
Blinsk
Churesh
Cheoni
Mountains

One

The Battle of Brandsveid, in which the combined armies of the Six Kingdoms met the monstrous army of Lord Brand to determine the future of Dis, was the event Vergil Parmeligo, Knight of the Order of the Unyielding Badger, had been waiting for his entire life. Never had there been a battle like this one. Seriously, this battle had everything: brave knights charging on horseback, goblin hordes, a giant battering ram, undead wraiths wielding enchanted swords, trolls, ogres, deception, subterfuge, betrayal... all the stuff that makes for a really epic battle. In addition to the mass killing, I mean. Unfortunately for Vergil, he slept through it.

More on that in a moment.

The Battle of Brandsveid is generally considered by historians to be the end of the Dark Age of Dis and the beginning of the Dissian Industrial Age. On the other hand, history is written by the victors[1], who are notorious for oversimplifying complex events. Battles make for convenient historical boundaries because they are (1) exciting and (2) easily pinpointed at a particular place and time, but a more accurate explanation of the rapid changes that characterized

---

[1] These days, Dissian historians are no longer required by law to be named Victor, but the term remains as a pejorative appellation for historians whose simplistic methods harken back to the legendary incompetence of their forebears.

Dis at this time would point to the discovery of the mysterious element known as zelaznium, without which the myriad technological advancements of the Industrial Age might never have occurred.[2]

Zelaznium is so valuable today, in fact, that it is hard to imagine that there was a time when a pouch full of the purest form of the silvery powder could be stolen from the laboratory of the court alchemist in Avaressa by a band of twenty goblins and carried out of the city in broad daylight. But that is exactly what happened—just twelve years before the Battle of Brandsveid.

Goblin raids were frequent enough in those days that the city guard no longer even affected a pretense of being able to repel them all; their usual response was to wait until the invaders had finished their plundering and then pursue them if the value of their booty warranted the risk and effort. In this particular case, all the invaders had taken was a small pouch of silvery dust that had apparently been left unsecured in the alchemist's laboratory, prompting little but shrugs from the guards who watched as the goblins paraded out of the city. In fact, the goblins would almost certainly have gotten away with their crime if they hadn't made the mistake of also absconding with the alchemist himself. Even so, the city guard were loath to risk their lives to recover one old man who spent his time in the basement of the palace burning his eyebrows off with potions, and thus the rescue of the great alchemist Zelaznus, discoverer of the element that was to change the course of the history of Dis, was left to the aforementioned knight-errant, Vergil, and his faithful squire Salivar.

Vergil Parmeligo was for many years a knight in name only, being the heir of a small but lucrative cucumber-farming estate just outside the city of Avaressa, the capital city of the Kingdom of

---

[2] The first known use of zelaznium was in the accursed Blades of Brakboorn, which were given to the kings of the Six Kingdoms, eventually transforming their owners into wraiths in his service. The first intentional attempt to harness the power of zelaznium, however, was the creation of the Mirrors of Milah. Both the Blades of Brakboorn and Mirrors of Milah were instrumental in bringing about the Battle of Brandsveid, which is recounted in detail in a previous volume of the history of Dis, titled *Disenchanted*.

Avaress. The estate had been established by his great-grandfather, who had accepted the knightship from the Count of the province of Balphry in lieu of payment for thirty Peraltian sheep. Knightships in Dis are not hereditary, technically speaking, but this particular title was renewed for each successive scion in Vergil's family, partly as a reconfirmation of the special relationship that existed between Vergil's family and that of the count, and partly because the alternative was to settle up for the now long-deceased sheep.

But while Vergil's forebears treated the knightship as little more than a standing invitation to the best parties, Vergil took his responsibilities as a knight seriously, spending countless hours learning to ride, joust and duel, with the help of his faithful man-servant Salivar. Although the management of the estate was ostensibly Vergil's responsibility, he found over time that it ran just as well without his interference, and as the years wore on, he spent more and more of his time reading books on chivalry and practicing what he took to be the habits and skills of a dutiful knight. His position as overseer of a small agricultural endeavor afforded him little opportunity to put the principles of chivalry into practice, however, and it was on his fortieth birthday that he decided to set out with Salivar (whom he had recently anointed as his squire) in search of a worthy quest to pursue.

At the time of the zelaznium theft, Vergil and Salivar had just spent a month traveling across western Avaress in search of adventure, but thus far had encountered nothing more challenging than deer ticks and saddle sores. Disappointed, they found themselves back in Avaressa, and when they heard that a tribe of goblins from the Wastes of Preel had made off with the court alchemist, they lost no time in pursuing the abductors.

The pair had been in pursuit for less than two hours when they encountered an elderly man lying battered and bloody on the side of the road. Intent on his quarry, Vergil was reluctant to tend to the man, but his chivalrous instincts won out by a slight margin over the dogged pursuit of his quest. He pulled back on the reins of his faithful steed, Penumbra, and held up his hand to Salivar, who rode close behind on his nag, Smelto. But as he regarded the man from Penumbra's back, it became clear to Vergil that he was beyond help;

they had arrived on the scene just in time to witness the man expire from his wounds.

"Hail, stranger," Vergil called from upon his steed. "Seeing you lying there upon the ground, I cannot but wish we had come upon you either somewhat sooner or somewhat later, for as a knight-errant in the service of the Order of the Unyielding Badger, it is incumbent upon me to offer assistance to those in need whom I might encounter on my travels. But as I regard you lying bloodied and broken by the roadside, I am led to the ineluctable conclusion that you are beyond help, and will shortly expire, with or without my help."

The old man nodded weakly. "I appreciate your candid assessment of my situation," he said, "which concurs with my own. Fortunately, I am by this point beyond pain and am merely awaiting the extinguishing of my spirit, at which point the fortunes of my material form will no longer be of any concern to me. I assume from your pace and stern countenance that you are en route to some important business, and I assure you that it is no bother for me to imagine that you came upon me ten minutes later, at which point you'd have found only a corpse, obliging you to do naught but say a prayer for my soul as you pass by."

"I am much gratified by your pragmatism," said Vergil. "For your deduction is correct: my faithful squire and I are hot on the trail of a band of goblins who abducted the court alchemist, a man known as Zelaznus, from the fair city of Avaressa. It is our intention to rescue said alchemist, return him to his post, and perhaps give these uncouth invaders a bit of a drubbing in the process."

"Ah, tis a noble mission indeed," replied the old man. "But now I must deliver some bad news to you: although your intentions are worthy and you are no doubt the best man for the job, your mission is doomed to fail. For this Zelaznus which you seek is no other than the man who lies, bloody and broken, on the roadside before you, speaking his last even now."

"By Grovlik!" cried Vergil. "This is then a harsh day for us both, for I shall fail in my first quest as a knight-errant and you shall shortly be no more."

"It would seem that fate has dealt us each a cruel hand this day," Zelaznus agreed. "However, there remains for you the possibility of amelioration of your failure, if not redemption. For although I hope that I have been of some service to the court of Avaress these past many years and my mind is still sharp, like all mortals I am allotted a limited number of days in which to toil. There are things that outlast men, however—discoveries that have the power to transform civilization. One of these, in the form of a pouch of silvery dust, is in the possession of those very goblins which you have been pursuing."

"A pouch of silver?" asked Vergil, dubiously. "I find it difficult to believe that even a very large sack filled with gold could 'transform civilization,' as you put it." Salivar nodded his assent.

"Not silver," Zelaznus gasped, rapidly weakening. "A mysterious element I recently discovered. If what I suspect about its properties is true, then this dust could be used to manufacture devices with capabilities bordering on magical."

"Such artifacts have existed in Dis for thousands of years," said Vergil. "History is full of accounts of the mischief caused by the magical talismans, such as the Purse of Priam and the Accursed Chamber Pot of Strambus."

"But in the past," Zelaznus interjected, his voice now so faint they had to lean forward in their saddles to hear him, "these artifacts were very rare and generally one of a kind—or of very limited issue, at least. Once the properties of this dust are fully documented, I believe it will be possible for simple tradesmen with minimal skill to manufacture seemingly magical devices by the thousand. Imagine an army of goblins equipped with devices that can be used to see right through enemy fortifications, or a dozen goblin chiefs able to communicate with each other over distances of hundreds of miles, in order to coordinate an attack on a human settlement."

Vergil and Salivar exchanged doubtful glances. Clearly the old alchemist had lapsed into delusion. His words were still coherent, but the ideas behind them were beyond ridiculous. Still, if the silvery powder was a tenth as powerful as Zelaznus indicated, it was worth retrieving from the goblins. And clearly the powder had some value, as it had apparently been the prime rationale for the goblin raid. Goblins were uncouth but preeminently practical: whether they had stolen the dust for their own purposes or on someone else's bidding, they had *some* reason for taking it, and the end result was unlikely to be beneficial to humanity.

"Sir knight, you cannot let the dust fall into the wrong hands," gasped Zelaznus, echoing Vergil's own thoughts. "If some aspiring tyrant or ambitious goblin chief masters the secrets of the powder...." He trailed off, unable to continue.

"We are in agreement, good sir," said Vergil. "If this strange powder is valuable enough for the goblins to steal it, that is reason enough to take it from them. By your leave, good Zelaznus, I will honor your impending death by continuing my pursuit of said monsters."

Zelaznus didn't reply, simply staring blankly back at Vergil.

"Not to rush things," said Vergil, "but the goblins recede from our grasp with each moment we spend in deliberation."

Zelaznus continued to stare.

"My liege," said Salivar, "I believe our friend has expired, thereby releasing you of any obligation to tend to his needs, which, if he still has any, are now beyond your bailiwick."

"Your perspicacity serves you well, faithful Salivar," said Vergil. "I see now that you are correct, and that what I took to be the dithering of an old man is in fact the lifeless stare of a corpse. Under more opportune circumstances, I would instruct you to return to Avaressa with the body to see to it that it receives a proper burial, but I'm afraid that I may require your assistance dealing with the brutes that have treated our late friend Zelaznus so roughly."

"I quite understand, my liege," said Salivar. "As loath as I am to leave an honorable man's body to be devoured by wolves and crows, duty requires that we continue our pursuit posthaste."

"Well said, faithful Salivar," replied Zelaznus. "Let us then honor our fallen friend by leaving his corpse to be torn apart by carrion beasts while we recover the pouch of which he spoke in his dying breaths."

Vergil gave Penumbra a kick, and the brave horse began again to trot down the path, with Salivar's mount Smelto following close behind, leaving Zelaznus to the elements.

It was shortly after sunset that the pair came upon the goblin camp, not far off the road. The goblins, evidently unaware or unafraid of being pursued, had made camp in an open field and even now were laughing and carrying on around a fire while their mounts grazed nearby. Vergil and Salivar had dismounted some distance back, secured their horses to a small shrub and then crept through the weeds toward the rollicking band. They watched silently from the shadows, assessing their options. Salivar thought it best to wait until the goblins fell asleep and sneak into their camp to quietly abscond with the powder, but Vergil argued otherwise.

"It is unbefitting one of my station to skulk about in the dark," said Vergil.

"You can leave the skulking to me," offered Salivar. "I shall sneak into the camp to retrieve the pouch while you remain hidden here in the dark, so that your reputation as a valiant and daring knight-errant can remain unsullied."

"That is an eminently reasonable suggestion, dear Salivar," said Vergil, "but I'm afraid that as usual, your understanding of the rigorous demands of the profession of knight-errant is faulty. I cannot sit idly by while you carry on like a common thief, tainting my chivalrous nature by association. No, we shall confront these goblins as men and demand that they return what they have stolen. For it is common knowledge that goblins are cowards whose bravado persists only as long as they significantly outnumber their enemies."

"And you don't consider a ten-to-one ratio a significant enough margin to allow them to maintain the appearance of bravery?"

"One hundred men are no match for a knight-errant and his dauntless squire," said Vergil.

"Perhaps," ventured Salivar, "the problem is that I am not as dauntless as you suppose."

"Nonsense, Salivar. Follow my lead and we shall have no trouble at all dealing with these boorish monsters. Think of them as wayward children desperate for moral guidance. You will see, dear Salivar. Creatures of weak mind cannot but bend their will to the irresistible force of a one well-schooled in the arts of chivalry. Now, follow me. And walk boldly. I'll countenance no skulking."

Vergil stood up straight and marched toward the goblin camp, with Salivar doing his best to follow in kind. So oblivious were the goblins that the pair were only a few paces from the clearing when one of them cried out. Several others suddenly turned to face the intruders, and a burly tattooed goblin whom Vergil took to be the leader began barking orders, warning the others to be on the lookout for additional intruders sneaking through the weeds. Salivar felt a surge of hope as he realized the genius of Vergil's plan: the goblins would assume that two men would only dare to approach the camp so bravely if the camp were secretly surrounded.

"You need not be alarmed," announced Vergil. "It is only the two of us. I am Vergil Parmeligo, Knight of the Order of the Unyielding Badger, and this is my faithful squire Salivar. We have come to demand that you return what you have stolen from the laboratory of the court alchemist of Avaressa, to wit: a pouch of silvery powder of mysterious origin and untold properties. Hand it over without delay and my companion and I will not slay you all in retribution for the murder of our friend, Zelaznus, whom you left for dead some miles back."

The chief nodded, seeming to consider Vergil's words carefully, then holding out his hand for Vergil to shake. "Your terms strike me as reasonable." he said, as they shook hands. "I am Khotem, chief of the Cholanthi tribe."

"Pleased to meet you, Chief Khotem," said Vergil, bowing slightly.

Khotem turned to a goblin sitting by the fire. "Etric, hand me the pouch we found at the alchemist's laboratory."

The goblin reached into the satchel at his side and pulled out a leather pouch no larger than a man's hand. He got up and handed it to the chief.

"And you promise to let us go?" Khotem asked Vergil, holding the pouch to his chest.

"I can make no assurances regarding the king or the authorities in Avaressa," said Vergil. "They may well seek vengeance for the death of the alchemist. Nor can I promise that I will be so merciful the next time we meet. I pledge only that we will leave your camp unmolested tonight and return to Avaressa with the pouch in the morning. If we travel quickly, we may still be able to recover the alchemist's corpse and see that he has a fitting burial."

Chief Khotem nodded again. "That seems more than fair, after all the trouble we've caused." he said. "If we had any idea how valuable this pouch is, we'd never have taken it in the first place. We are, after all, mere goblins with no appreciation of such delicate matters."

"You are quite sensible for an abominable hybrid of beast and man," said Vergil. He turned to Salivar. "You see, my faithful squire, there is no need for skulking about when one has purity of heart and strength of will. Our friend Chief Khotem, brute though he is, instinctively knows when he is in the presence of his superior."

Salivar nodded, impressed with his liege's wisdom in matters of diplomacy.

Khotem held out his hand, and Vergil reached out to take the pouch from him. But as Vergil's fingers neared the pouch, Khotem flicked his wrist, launching the pouch over Vergil's head. Vergil spun around in time to see another goblin catch it.

"See here," said Vergil. "We had a deal. Hand me the pouch before I become cross."

The goblin feigned handing the pouch to Vergil and tossed it back over his head to Khotem.

"Blast you!" snapped Vergil, turning back to Khotem. "Cease these childish games. If you do not hand over the pouch this instant, I am revoking my offer of immunity. If I have to take it by force, I will kill every last one of you!"

"I'm sorry," said Khotem, with a smile. "I couldn't resist. Here, please take the pouch with my sincere apologies."

"Yes, well," said Vergil, reaching for the pouch again. "I suppose I can—"

This time, Khotem tossed the pouch over the fire to a goblin sitting cross-legged on the other side.

"That's it!" growled Vergil, drawing his sword and taking a step toward the fire. "I demand that you hand over the pouch right now!"

"Here you go," said the goblin holding the pouch, and made as if to toss it to Vergil. But it sailed over Vergil's head, out of his reach. Chief Khotem caught it.

"This is disgraceful!" cried Vergil. "This sort of behavior is why your kind lead a desperate, nomadic existence on the outskirts of the Wastes of Preel, rather than—" He leaped into the air as Khotem tossed the pouch over his head again. It passed within an inch of the outstretched fingers of his left hand. Vergil turned to Salivar, who stood by helplessly. "Blast you, Salivar! Help me!"

Being of stout build and a good five inches shorter than Vergil, Salivar was not a particularly good candidate to offer assistance under the circumstances, but he nodded and lumbered around the fire toward the goblin called Etric, who now held the pouch. As Salivar neared Etric, however, another goblin sitting near the fire stuck out his foot, tripping him. Salivar fell face-first onto the dirt in front of Etric, provoking a round of guffaws from the goblins.

"Sorry about that," said Etric. "We're just having a little fun." He held the pouch in front of Salivar's face. But as Salivar reached out to take it, he threw it back over the fire toward the goblin behind Vergil.

By this time Vergil was overcome with rage and no longer thinking clearly. As the pouch soared through the air toward the goblin, he swung at it with the flat of his blade, hoping to knock it to the ground. But the tip of his sword caught on the side of the pouch, tearing it wide open. The powder poured out of the opening and dispersed in the breeze, enveloping Vergil in a silvery cloud. Unthinking, Vergil gasped at the sight, inhaling a lungful of the powder as the mostly empty pouch fell to the ground in front of him. The goblins stared in shock as Vergil stood coughing and blinking in the dissipating cloud. "Now see what you've—" he started, and then fell to the ground, unconscious.

Two

The next sensation of which Vergil was consciously aware was an eruption of pain in his left thigh, just above the knee. He screamed and jerked awake, finding himself sitting bolt upright in a bed. After a moment it came to him that this bed was his own, and that he was in his bedroom in his family's home just outside Avaressa. Whatever had happened with the goblins, all seemed to be well now—except for the portly, mustachioed man who was currently dragging a rusty bowsaw across Vergil's left thigh just above the knee, the dull teeth tearing into his flesh. Vergil screamed again.

At Vergil's second outburst, the man looked up from his work, seemingly puzzled to find the limb he was attempting to sever attached to a screaming man. "Get away from me!" cried Vergil, his voice a hoarse whisper, batting weakly at the man's hands. "Stop that!"

The man's mouth fell open. His face had gone pale with fear or shock and his right hand was white-knuckled on the saw that still rested on Vergil's thigh. Blood dripped down the side of Vergil's leg.

"Kindly remove your saw from my thigh," growled Vergil through gritted teeth.

The man nodded dumbly and lifted the saw. A new wave of pain shot through Vergil's leg, and he sucked in air through his teeth to avoid screaming again. With the pressure released, blood now flowed freely from the wound. Fortunately the saw had been dull enough that it hadn't penetrated much below the skin.

"What in Grovlik's name do you think you're doing?" demanded Vergil, his voice still barely a whisper. He felt oddly drained, as if he was recovering from a long illness, and the skin of his exposed leg seemed strangely pale. Maybe it was just the contrast with the blood flowing from the fresh wound, but the leg itself seemed somehow foreign—withered and drawn, like the leg of an old man.

"Good heavens," said the portly man at last, letting the saw drop to the floor with a clatter. "You're awake!" The man sat on a wooden chair, his prominent belly spilling out beneath a badly tailored tunic. His hairy arms, vaguely pear-like shape, and round, bulbous features put Vergil in mind of a gorilla.

"Your powers of observation are as sharp as your saw," growled Vergil. "Who are you and why were you attempting to saw off my leg?"

"I beg your forgiveness, m'lord," said the man, pushing his chair back and bowing low. "My name is Handri. I'm the caretaker here at the estate—well, *your* estate, I guess. I've been charged with your care."

"You lie," said Vergil. "The caretaker of my estate is a man named Galbard, and, I might add, he has never once attempted to saw any of my limbs off."

"I'm afraid Galbard doesn't, um, work here anymore," said Handri, standing upright again. His wiry, hairy arms hung, slightly bent, at his side, accentuating his simian appearance. "I'm the current caretaker."

"I see," said Vergil, unconvinced. "And tell me, Handri the current caretaker, did something in your obviously very comprehensive training prompt you to think I required pruning?"

As the blood continued to pour down Vergil's leg, he moved to get out of bed, but was suddenly overcome with light-headedness and nearly lost consciousness again. His joints were sore and his muscles were weak, as if he hadn't moved for weeks. What had happened to him?

"Don't try to get up!" Handri cried, holding up his hands in alarm. "Wait here. I'll get some rags to bandage that leg." Before Vergil could think of anything to say, the man hurriedly left the room.

Moving slowly so as not to pass out, Vergil propped up his pillows and leaned back to survey the room. Except for a thick layer of dust on all the furniture, it looked just as it had the morning he had set out on his journey with Salivar. How long had he been sleeping, for so much dust to have collected? It had to have been weeks, at least. It certainly hadn't seemed that long, though. Other than the dust on the furniture and the sunlight streaming through the window, the only thing that gave him a sense that any time had passed was the dim memory of a dream he'd had, perhaps minutes or hours earlier. The details now eluded him, but a sense of foreboding remained. A gigantic, vaguely humanoid monster of some sort had threatened all of Dis, and only Vergil could stop it. But before he could recall any more, Handri returned to the room with a glass bottle of clear liquid and a handful of rags. He pulled a chair up to Vergil's bedside, and unstoppered the bottle. Before Vergil could ask what was in it, he began pouring the liquid onto Vergil's leg. Vergil screamed again, despite his best efforts. Whatever was in the bottle hurt more than the saw had.

"What *is* that?" he gasped.

"Disinfectorant," said Handri, staring at Vergil as if the word was supposed to mean something. "For killing the germs."

"The *what?*" asked Vergil, trembling.

"Tiny bugs that make infections," said Handri, pinching his fingers together. "Too small to see."

Vergil stared at him in horror. If seeing Handri trying to saw his leg off hadn't already convinced Vergil of the man's insanity, he was certainly convinced now. Vergil tried to snatch the bottle away from him, but nearly passed out again. He fell back against the pillows and moaned. He was at Handri's mercy.

"Forgive me for questioning your skills as a caretaker," he managed to say, "if that is indeed who you are. But I am not a rosebush, for Grovlik's sake. I do not believe tiny bugs should be our primary concern at this point."

"But they're everywhere!" Handri protested. "I learnt it in my training. On the bed, on your skin, in the air…."

"Please," Vergil groaned. "I do not know what kind of superstitious nonsense they taught you in caretaker school, but I can tell you there are no tiny bugs in, on, or around my leg. As I am nigh immobilized and in need of medical attention thanks to your overzealous gardening, I seem to have little choice but to trust you with my immediate care, but you are to take no further action directed at eliminating tiny bugs on my person. Do you understand?"

"Yes, but the bugs can make—"

"There are no tiny bugs!" Vergil moaned. "They do not exist! And if you were worried about tiny bugs getting into my wound, maybe you shouldn't have tried to *cut my leg off.*"

"I said I was sorry for that," Handri muttered. "You don't have to keep bringing it up."

"Forget it," groaned Vergil, too weak to argue. "Just promise me you are not going to put any more of that stuff on my leg. It is my leg, and I am not obligated to indulge your ridiculous superstitions about invisible bugs."

"Okay," said Handri. "But if the—"

"Not another word!" cried Vergil. "No more talk about tiny bugs. Promise me."

Handri sighed heavily and looked at Vergil's wound, which was still bubbling and fizzing from the substance Handri had poured on it. "I promise. No more talk about tiny bugs."

"Good," said Vergil. "Now, bandage up my leg before I bleed to death. And make it nice and snug, to keep the evil spirits out."

Handri grumbled something Vergil didn't catch, but he dutifully began bandaging Vergil's leg. Vergil had a thousand questions to ask, but if Handri was as dim as he seemed, he would need all his concentration to keep from screwing up the dressing. Still, Vergil had to admit the man was good with his hands. He reminded Vergil somewhat of Salivar: not conventionally intelligent, but capable in his own way.

Handri finished wrapping the wound, and Vergil gave him an approving nod. Actually thanking the man seemed a bit much, considering that he had caused the wound in the first place, but he saw no harm in a little positive reinforcement. "A passable job," Vergil said, appraising the dressing.

Handri pouted. "Just don't expect me to amputate your leg if it gets infectorated."

"Under no circumstances will I expect you to amputate my leg," said Vergil. "In fact, I forbid it, as you have already made one unsolicited attempt."

"That was for your own good," Handri protested.

"Really," said Vergil. "Perhaps, alleged caretaker, you could explain to me how you expected me to benefit from the loss of a perfectly good leg."

"It's kind of a long story," said Handri.

"I have time," said Vergil. "I appear to have been in this bed for several weeks already, so I assume I have already missed any engagements I may have had on my calendar." He had been staring at the skin on the back of his hands, which was loose and wrinkled, and exceptionally pale except for a number of dark blotches. What kind of illness had done this to him? And would he ever recover?

"Not weeks," Handri said quietly, his eyes downcast.

"What?" asked Vergil. "How long have I been asleep? More than a few days, unless that dust is your idea of decor. Months?"

Handri bit his lip. "Maybe I should get Lord Balphry."

"Lord Balphry?" asked Vergil. "You refer to my liege, Mallech, the Count of Balphry?"

"I…" began Handri. "Maybe I should let Lord Balphry explain. Please, if I send word for him now, he can be here by tomorrow. I'm sure he'll want to——"

"How long, Handri?" Vergil asked again.

"Well, I don't know *exactly*," said Handri, pulling a small silvery object from his pocket. He flipped open a tiny door on the object with his thumb and squinted at it. "But as near as I can figure, you've been asleep for…" His eyes drifted to the ceiling and his lips moved as he silently worked numbers in his head. While Vergil waited, he took notice of his own hands. He rotated them slowly in front of his eyes, taking in the wrinkles the sagging skin, the dark splotches. He realized now that they looked like the hands of a much older man. Handri continued, "One hundred three years, twenty-six days, fourteen hours and nine minutes."

Vergil dropped his hands to his lap and stared at Handri, trying to determine whether the man was joking. But there was no sign of humor in the man's face.

"Did you say a hundred *years*?"

"One hundred and three," Handri repeated. "Or so."

"That's impossible," said Vergil, looking at his hands and arms again. "I'd be long dead. This is some sort of trick."

"No trick, m'lord," said Handri. "I am the fifth caretaker to watch over your estate since you got here. Galbard was the first. I have been told that many doctors attempted to revive you, but they could not. The man who was caretaker before me told me that you had breathed in a whole lot of zelaznium, and that it slowed down your, um, what's it called? Metabolism. Put you into a coma and made you age slower. Nobody else thought you would ever wake up, but I knew you would. I mean, I always hoped; that's why I took this job. You were my hero when I was a child. The last real knight-errant, his career tragically ended while trying to preserve the secret of zelaznium. But I didn't know for sure that you were going to wake up until recently."

Vergil remembered inhaling the cloud of silvery powder, which Handri was calling zelaznium—a clear reference to the dying alchemist, Zelaznus, whom Vergil and Salivar had met on the roadside. It was hard to say how much of what Handri told him was factual, but that part, at least, rang true. "Oh?" said Vergil skeptically. "And how did you know?"

"Your, um, waste," said Handri. "What was in it. Or rather, what isn't."

"What in Dis are you talking about?"

"Zelaznium," said Vergil. "It, um, comes out of you. Slowly, ever since you got here. It's a secret passed on from one caretaker to the next. And between you and me, it's the only reason you're still alive. I pay for everything to take care of this estate with your uh, you-know-what."

Vergil regarded Handri dubiously. "To be clear, you're saying I literally have zelaznium coming out of my…"

"Yes, m'lord. Over the past few weeks, though, there hasn't been much of it. If the zelaznium was keeping you in a coma, and you were running out of it, I figured it made sense you would wake up when it was gone. I thought it would be a few more weeks, though. Didn't expect it to happen while I was cutting your leg off. That was my mistake."

Vergil began to laugh. "Now I know this is a joke," he said. "Even if that story were not completely ridiculous, which it is, my family has numerous profitable holdings in this area. Enough to maintain this estate and its staff for well over a hundred years."

Handri shrugged. "I don't know anything about that. For as long as I've been here, we've had to get by on our own. There used to be a lot of servants, I guess, but that was long before I started. These days it's just me. I raise a few crops and sell most of the produce at the market, but we don't get any money from your family's other holdings. I've asked Lord Balphry about this many times, but he says he can't spare anything to help."

Vergil frowned. If Handri was playing his part in some sort of elaborate joke, he was an exceedingly good actor, and he'd been coached in great detail. And the throbbing in Vergil's leg was a testament to how committed he was to the part.

"To clarify," said Vergil, "when you say 'Lord Balphry,' you mean Mallech, the Count of Balphry?"

"No, m'lord. His great-grandson, Marko."

"His great-grandson?" said Vergil. "But Mallech has no...." He stared at the simple, guileless face of Handri. It was becoming very hard to believe this was all some kind of ruse. But if Handri was telling the truth, then Mallech had gotten married and had at least one son while Vergil had been asleep. And that son had had a son, and *that* son was the current Lord Balphry. Vergil's mind rebelled at the idea that all of this could have transpired in what seemed to him almost no time at all, but neither could he bring himself to believe that the simple-minded man sitting in front of him was lying.

"So... it's true?" he said at last. "I really have been asleep for a hundred years?"

"A hundred and three and change," said Handri, smiling. "It's a record, I think."

Vergil closed his eyes, trying to make the words mean something, but the throbbing in his leg kept bringing him back to the present. He looked at Handri. "That still doesn't explain why you tried to cut my leg off," he said.

"Oh, right," said Handri. "I thought there might still be some usable zelaznium in your body. This whole place is falling apart and the last of our food stores is almost gone. I haven't been able to get enough zelaznium out of your waste for the past few weeks to pay for basic supplies. So it was either start cutting your limbs off or starve. I figured you didn't need your leg, since you never got out of bed anyway."

"You said you knew I was going to wake up."

"Yep," Handri said, beaming.

"So you were going to cut off my leg, even though you knew I was going to wake up."

"Right," said Handri. "I told you, you weren't using it."

"But I would need it when I woke up."

Handri opened his mouth and then closed it again, rubbing his chin. "You know what?" he said. "You're right, Sir. I didn't really think that through."

Vergil sighed. "Well, unfortunately for us both, I did wake up, so I am afraid I'm going to need my leg. And now that I am awake, we can go see Lord Balphry and clear up these questions about my estate's finances. I can't be living in a house that is falling apart." He slowly swung his legs over the side of the bed and placed his feet on the floor. He was wearing silk pajamas, and the left leg had been slit wide open—presumably by Handri. Vergil was struck again by how pale and gaunt his limbs looked. Dizziness nearly overcame him, and he found himself leaning against Handri to keep from falling over.

"Please, m'lord," said Handri. "Don't push yourself. You're in no shape to be walking around."

Vergil realized he was right. If Handri was to be believed, he'd been bedridden for a very long time. But just how badly had he deteriorated? "Do you have... a mirror?" Vergil gasped.

"Yes," said Handri. "Can you sit?"

Vergil nodded weakly, sitting up and releasing his hold on Handri.

After making sure that Vergil wasn't going to topple over, Handri got up and darted out of the room again. He returned a moment later with a hand-held mirror. He sat down on the chair, clutching the mirror to his chest. "Are you sure you want to do this now?" he asked. "You've already had a shock today."

"Are you referring to me waking up after a hundred years or you trying to saw my leg off?"

"I said I was sorry!"

"Just hand me the mirror."

"Alright," said Handri. "But you know what they say. Looks can be deceiving. Technically, you're over a hundred and forty years old, but nobody knows what the zelaznium actually did to you. So maybe, even though you look—"

"The mirror, Handri!"

Handri bit his lip and handed Vergil the mirror. Vergil grabbed it and held it up to his face without hesitation. He was a knight-errant in the service of the Order of the Unyielding Badger, by Grovlik. He had no fear of goblins, ogres or trolls; he certainly wasn't going to be afraid of his own reflection, no matter how many years had passed.

But as he brought the mirror in front of his face, his first thought was that there was something wrong with it. For rather than showing his own face, it showed that of some pathetic, wrinkled old man, with wispy white hair, dark bags under his eyes and skin sagging at the jowls. He almost burst into laughter, but his amusement quickly turned to horror. Underneath that pallid, flaccid skin was a face he recognized.

"No," he whispered. "It can't be…"

"It's not so bad," said Handri. "You actually look pretty good for a hundred and forty-three. A little sunshine and exercise and you could pass for seventy."

The room began to spin, and the mirror fell from Vergil's fingers. The sound of it shattering on the floor was the last sound he heard before passing out.

Three

Vergil slept for most of the next three days. He wouldn't have thought he'd needed it after a century in bed, but the slightest physical exertion completely wore him out. He reassured himself that, despite his ancient appearance, his weakness and lack of endurance were mainly the result of muscle atrophy and not simply old age. Clearly he hadn't aged at a normal rate while asleep, or he'd have died decades earlier. So how old was he really? Not forty, certainly. But not a hundred and forty-three either. *I'm only as old as I feel*, he thought, trying out the phrase as a sort of mantra. But as he stood, sweaty and trembling, leaning against the door to his room, wondering if he could make it back to his bed again, he decided he didn't need a mantra quite yet.

Handri nursed him back to some semblance of health over the next week. At first, he could eat only broth and a little porridge, which was good, because according to Handri, that was about all that was left in the pantry. Vergil wondered how Handri managed to maintain his pear-like physique under such privation, but eventually concluded it was simply the way the man was built. It wasn't for lack of exercise, certainly. In addition to caring for Vergil, Handri spent many hours a day working around the estate, clearing the weeds and brush that constantly threatened to overtake the estate, working in the garden, and engaging in various makeshift and mostly futile repairs of the mansion. Vergil's enthusiasm about finally having the strength to take a tour of the estate was tempered by the realization of just how bad the condition of the estate was. His father would have been appalled to see it like this, and he had a hard time believing any heir of Mallech would deliberately have allowed it to fall into such disrepair.

As Handri told it, Mallech had taken temporary charge of the estate shortly after Vergil had lapsed into a coma. Vergil had no heirs, and his own family had been killed in a goblin raid when he was just a boy, so it made sense that responsibility for the estate had "temporarily" fallen to Vergil's nominal liege. But as with Vergil's knightship, the custodianship had been passed from one generation to the next, and for all practical purposes Vergil's holdings were now the possession of Marko, the current Lord Balphry.

When Vergil left on his quest, the estate had been an almost-self-sufficient farm, and whatever the family and resident servants couldn't produce they could easily procure by trading crops or livestock in the city. Any reasonably competent manager should have had no trouble paying for the upkeep of the estate as well as Vergil's own care. This meant either that this current Lord Balphry was remarkably incompetent or something else had happened to undermine the estate's profitability. Vergil had made the obvious assumption that the ever-present threat of goblins had finally gotten the better of the estate; his family had lost a lot of chickens and goats to the little monsters during his tenure as overseer. But Handri didn't seem to be aware of any goblin threat, and in fact seemed quite uncomfortable with Vergil's questions about the current state of the goblin menace. When Vergil pressed him for answers about the estate's decline, he would simply shake his head and say "Estates like this don't make money anymore"—an answer that was as unsatisfying as it was circular.

Two weeks after Vergil awoke, they set off to see Marko, who lived on a much larger estate about twenty miles to the east. Handri expressed doubts as to whether Vergil was up to the journey, but Vergil insisted he was, and in any case the pantry was now completely empty, so they didn't have much choice but to throw themselves on the mercy of Marko. However much had changed in the past century, surely the aristocracy still looked after its own. At least, that was Vergil's hope—the condition of his estate to the contrary.

They had no horses to ride. According to Handri, the stables had been empty for the past forty years, at least. Vergil assumed this meant they would have to walk to Marko's estate, but Handri, claiming to have a better idea, ran off to one of the sheds on the periphery of the property. While Vergil waited on the porch, trying to prepare himself mentally for the day's journey, Handri returned, wheeling some sort of steel-framed contraption toward him.

"What in Grovlik's name is that?" asked Vergil.

Handri frowned. "You've never seen a bicycle before?"

"*Bi*-cycle," Vergil said, pronouncing the word slowly. "Because of the two wheels, I suppose. What do you do with it?"

"Why, you ride it, of course," said Handri. "Watch." He threw his left leg over the frame of the thing, placing his round rump on a padded triangular seat and his left foot on a pedal connected to some sort of gear system. He then pushed off with his right foot, and Vergil watched in amazement as the portly figure glided away down the packed dirt road. His feet were working the pedals, moving a chain that connected to a gear attached to the rear wheel.

"What a wonderful contraption!" cried Vergil. "Why, it should be no trouble at all to trade such a marvelous curiosity for a proper horse!"

"What?" cried Handri, circling around back toward Vergil. "No, we're not going to trade it for a horse. We're going to ride them. There's another in the barn for you."

"You cannot be serious," said Vergil, scowling. "A knight-errant in the service of the Order of the Unyielding Badger cannot be seen riding such a contraption. It isn't dignified."

Handri skidded to a halt in front of him. "Lots of people ride them," he said.

"Not I," said Vergil.

Handri frowned, ruminating on the matter. "Well, I don't know much about the requirements of being a knight-errant," he said after a moment, "but I don't know why anyone would want to be one if they don't let you ride bicycles."

"It is not a *requirement*," Vergil explained. "But it is important that knights-errant maintain an air of respectability."

"Okay," said Handri. "Then I suppose we can walk, but it will take a lot longer. We'll have to beg for food and probably sleep in a ditch tonight, but I'm willing to make the sacrifice to spare your dignity."

Vergil rubbed his beard thoughtfully. "You say there's another bi-cycle in the barn?"

Less than an hour later, they were on the road. Despite his age, Vergil was relieved to find that he remained in possession of most of his coordination and reflexes, and he had little difficulty mastering the bicycle. It still seemed like an undignified way to travel, but he found the sensation of wind whipping past his face oddly enjoyable. It was like being on a horse without the jarring motion and copious excrement. They had to stop frequently to allow Vergil to rest, but they made good time, traveling on an old country road that connected the estates to the north of Avaressa. Vergil found himself constantly scanning the tree line for the signs of goblin brigands, but Handri seemed unconcerned. Of the two of them, only Vergil was armed; he had slung a rusty old sword across his back, despite Handri's vociferous protests. Handri seemed convinced that carrying a sword was somehow more likely to cause trouble than to solve it, but the logic of this notion escaped Vergil, and he chalked it up to the man's general obtuseness.

They took their first break less than half an hour after they set out, but this was occasioned not so much by Vergil's fatigue as by his curiosity. For running across the dirt road in front of them was something he had never seen before: a pair of metal rails, spaced maybe five feet apart, resting on top of a series of thick wooden beams. The beams were spaced a foot or so apart, and the spaces between them were filled with gravel. This strange road—if that's what it was—ran from the southwest to the northeast, and extended as far as Vergil could see in both directions. He couldn't be certain, but he thought the rails were vibrating slightly.

"What in Dis is this?" Vergil asked, standing between the rails.

"Oh," replied Handri, taking notice of Vergil's bafflement. "You've never seen a railroad before, have you? It's a sort of... well, it looks like you're about to see."

Vergil scowled at Handri, but followed his gaze down the tracks. In the distance, a black speck on the horizon was getting slowly larger. They watched it for some time.

"You'll want to get off the tracks," said Handri, who stood several feet away.

Vergil grunted, but didn't reply. He was beginning to resent being forced to rely on the dull-witted Handri as his guide to this strange new world. He watched as the object in the distance continued to approach. The vibration of the tracks increased, and he could now hear a low rumbling in the distance.

"Is that smoke?" he asked, peering at the haze that lingered in the distance.

"Steam," said Handri. "Well, and smoke too, I guess. It burns coal to boil water."

"This is a mobile water-boiling machine?" asked Vergil dubiously, watching the thing approach. It was difficult to judge the size of it, but it was clearly at least the width of the tracks and maybe twice as tall. "What is the point of that? Are they delivering soup?"

"No, the boiling water makes the train go. They're delivering coal, most likely. That train is going to Brandsveid."

"And what will Brandsveid do with the coal?"

"They burn it to make all sorts of things. Like trains, for instance."

"They burn coal to boil water to make the train go to bring coal to Brandsveid so they can burn it to make more trains?"

"Yep," said Handri. "It's called capitalism."

Vergil shook his head. "What a tremendous waste of—" As he spoke, a piercing howl sounded in the distance, causing him to jump. "Good grief, Handri, what was that? It startled me nearly out of my wits."

"The driver has seen you," said Handri. "He's warning you to get out of the way."

"Oh he is, is he?" Vergil. "We'll see about that. My sword, Handri!" He had left his sword lying in its scabbard against his bicycle, a few yards away.

"Sir?"

"My sword!" Vergil cried again. "I'll not let some son-of-a-cobbler train driver intimidate me. I'm a knight of the Order of the Unyielding Badger. Protocol must be observed!" He was nearly shouting now to be heard over the roaring of the train. Its whistle sounded again, but Vergil stood his ground.

Handri looked nervously from the train to Vergil and back. "Sir," he pleaded. "I'm sure the engineer means no disrespect. I doubt he's aware of your social status."

"My bearing alone should be indication enough for him," yelled Vergil. "And if he has any doubts, he should halt his infernal contraption and address me directly. I shall teach this upstart cur some manners!" He shook his fist at the train, and the whistle blew again in response. It showed no signs of slowing.

"Please, sir!" Handri howled. "I'm sure the driver would stop if he could, but he cannot! The train's momentum is too great!"

"Nonsense, Handri!" Vergil shouted. "Watch and you shall see. When the driver senses my indomitable will, he will have no choice but to stop." He folded his arms across his chest and thrust his chin into the air. The whistle blew again. The train was now less than a stone's throw away and closing quickly. The ground shook from its approach, and the roar of its wheels was like thunder. It occurred to Vergil that the train might not, after all, bow to his indomitable will. Realizing it was too late to move, he clamped his eyes shut and braced for impact.

The next thing Vergil knew, he was lying on the ground next to the tracks, with Handri on top of him and the train roaring past.

"Get off me, you fool!" Vergil cried. "First you attempt to rid me of my limbs, and now you rob me of my dignity!"

"I saved your life!" shouted Handri. "That train would have flattened you!"

Vergil scowled and shoved Handri off, then got to his feet. He brushed himself off and walked some distance away, where the sound of the train was less deafening. He sat down on a fallen log and Handri walked over and sat next to him. They watched as the rest of the train roared past.

"Goodness, Handri," shouted Vergil, after some time. "How long *is* this thing?"

"They are often fifty cars or more," Handri shouted back.

"What a nightmarish mode of transport," Vergil muttered.

"What?" Handri shouted.

But Vergil didn't reply. He simply stared as the cars rolled past. "What is that?" he asked, pointing at a crude drawing on the side of one of the cars. He had seen the same thing on several other cars—some sort of insignia. It was hard to tell with the cars moving so fast, but it looked to him like the head of a rodent.

"Huh?" said Handri. Another car passed, and Vergil pointed to the insignia, which had been painted onto this one as well. "Ah," said Handri. "That's Chiga Varra. He was some kind of revolutionary goblin leader, back in my grandparents' day. Young kids like to paint that picture on trains and bridges and such."

A few more cars passed, and Vergil caught sight of another one with the painting on it. Now that Handri had mentioned it, it did look like the head of a goblin. It was the hair that had thrown him off: a wild mane of bushy black hair that seemed to be blowing in the wind. The goblin's chin was thrust upwards, with an air of rakish defiance.

The train at last came to an end, and they watched it disappear to the northeast.

"I don't think I like the looks of that rakish goblin," said Vergil.

"He's long dead," said Handri. "No need to fear him."

"I fear no goblin!" snapped Vergil. "But he must have some symbolic importance, if people are still defacing train cars with his likeness."

Handri shrugged. "I don't think it means anything. Just bored kids."

Vergil shook his head. Any youngster he caught painting the likeness of a goblin leader on the side of a train would get a lesson in history—and a switch to his backside. "We have rested here long enough," he said. They crossed the railroad tracks to retrieve their bicycles and continued on their way.

By mid-afternoon they had reached a fork in the road which Vergil recognized as the halfway point between his own estate and that of Lord Balphry. Vergil found himself coasting to a halt at the fork, looking down the ill-maintained path to the left.

"This way, sir," said Handri, continuing down the right-hand path. But when Vergil remained still, Handri braked and circled back toward him.

"What is it, sir?" asked Handri. "Lord Balphry's estate is that way." He pointed to the right-hand path. "There is nothing down this path but a long-abandoned farmhouse. If your thought is to camp there for the night, I wouldn't recommend it, as the roof has largely fallen in and the place is home to any number of rodents and other pests. Besides, we should have no trouble reaching Lord Balphry's estate before dark."

But Vergil ignored him, and set off down the leftward path. He knew it was probably a bad idea, but he had to see it, if only to confirm the truth in his mind. Handri sighed but followed without further protest. The path was barely traversable thanks to the encroachment of vegetation, and after a couple of miles they had to abandon their bikes and walk the rest of the way, Vergil hacking his way through the underbrush with the sword. In another half-mile, they reached the house.

Vergil's heart sank as he saw it; the place was in even worse shape than Handri's description indicated. It seemed to be little more than a foundation with suggestions of walls protruding more-or-less vertically from it. It was hard to believe the house of Eucerine had fallen into such disrepair after only a hundred years.

"By Grovlik," Vergil gasped, falling to his knees from a combination of shock and fatigue. "What happened to this place?"

"It has been in ruins as long as I can remember," replied Handri.

Vergil surveyed the ruins. The passage of time alone could not explain the extent of the damage. Scorch marks and shattered glass attested to a more brutal and sudden form of destruction.

"These estates just don't make money anymore," said Handri. "The place probably fell into disrepair when the people who live here were forced to leave to find jobs in the city."

"Forced?" asked Vergil. "By whom?"

Handri shook his head. "It's not like that," he said. "Nobody forced them to leave, just like nobody forced people to leave *your* estate. These places, little independent farms and ranches, they just don't..."

"Just don't make money anymore," finished Vergil. "That's the extent of your knowledge of how the world works, isn't it? It never occurs to you to look for root causes. You see a house with the roof caving in, and you think 'Well, that's what houses do.'"

"Well, it is," said Handri. "Isn't it?"

"No!" cried Vergil, getting to his feet. "Many of these old estates have stood for hundreds of years! They don't just fall down, not without a reason."

"And you think you know the reason?"

"I do," said Vergil, stepping through the weeds and surveying the destruction. "For although clearly much has changed while I slept, the culprit here is the same creeping rot that has gnawed at the edges of human civilization for millennia. No, my benighted friend, this is not the sort of passive dilapidation characterized by the ravages of time, but rather the active destruction caused by a malevolent force that seeks to tear down all that is good and beautiful in the world, a force so potent that through pure volition it brought forth from the muck pits a race of brutes devoid of thought or feeling except hatred, anger and the urge to destroy."

"Sir," said Handri, "if you're speaking of—"

"Goblins!" exclaimed Vergil. "I see the signs, even decades later. Weather and weeds have done their part to cover up the evidence, but make no mistake, Handri, a melee occurred here. Goblins came down from the hills and slaughtered the residents of this estate. Members of the same accursed race that kidnapped old Zelaznus and thwarted my attempt to rescue him, putting me into a century-long sleep. Their kind must answer for these crimes!"

"I'm sure you are correct in your deduction," said Handri, "but if this place was ruined by goblins, it happened many years before I was born, for I never heard tell of it. And you have to understand that things have changed since then. It isn't fair to hold goblins as a race responsible for something that happened a hundred years ago."

"Not fair?" cried Vergil. "Is the mere passage of time sufficient to wash away guilt? A great crime took place here, Handri, and the fact that apparently no one remembers the nature of this slaughter makes me not less angry but more so! You speak to me of fairness, but what of justice, Handri? Were these goblin marauders ever held to account for their crimes?"

"Not to my knowledge, sir. But those goblins are long dead."

"And their descendants live on, having benefited from the crimes of their forebears. Is that *fair*, Handri? Is it fair that these murdering miscreants went on to spawn more of their kind while an entire family, including women and children, were cut down? I knew this family, and they did not deserve to die like this."

"I'm sure not," said Handri, "but I don't see that there's much to be done about it now. And while I'm not an expert on history, as I understand it the goblins didn't have much choice."

Vergil stared at Handri, appalled. "What are you saying, Handri?"

"Just that, um," Handri said uncertainly, "the goblins were here first. People moved in, built these big estates on their land, and the goblins had no place to go. So they struck back, trying to drive the humans from the frontiers. I'm not making excuses for the goblins, but the people who built these estates knew there were goblins here when they moved in."

"The people who settled this land were furthering the cause of civilization!" Vergil roared. "They are to be commended for their efforts at exterminating sub-humans, not condemned!"

Handri winced at this, but didn't seem to want to argue the point. "I'm just saying, they knew what they were getting into."

Vergil glared at him. "The family that built this estate had a daughter. She was only four years old when they started building. She lived her entire life on this estate. Tell me, Handri, did she 'know what she was getting into?'"

"Well, no," admitted Handri. "I don't suppose it's fair to hold a child responsible for the actions of her parents. That would be indecent."

"Exactly!" exclaimed Vergil. "She was completely innocent. The most innocent girl you could ever meet, in fact. Her name was Favorita." Vergil smiled, recalling the girl's rosy cheeks and golden hair. He sat down on a remnant of a wall and motioned for Handri to do the same. "Sit a moment with me, Handri, and I shall tell you of Favorita."

Handri sat.

"Never was a more beautiful woman seen in all of Dis," said Vergil, a rapturous expression on his face. "But Favorita's beauty was the least of her charms. She was exceedingly kind and generous, and possessed of such a formidable intelligence that she might have been the match of any man in a game of wits, were it not unseemly for the weaker sex to engage in such pursuits. Ah, but Handri, I have spoken of Favorita's innocence, and that is the quality that endeared her to her admirers the most. Handsome and wealthy gentlemen came from many leagues away to woo her, but she sent them all away without even a kiss for their troubles. Favorita was clearly sympathetic to these young men, but she insisted that she was holding out for a knight—and not just any knight, but one worthy of the title. So she sent all these men away disappointed. But none of them were more disappointed than Favorita herself, who despaired of ever finding her worthy knight. Her best friend, a buxom young servant girl named Jasmeen, attempted to console her, but to no avail. After each of these visits, Favorita's disconsolate moans could be heard late into the night, and often Jasmeen was so moved by her friend's sorrow that she joined in the moaning as well."

"That is a sad story indeed," said Handri.

"Yes," agreed Vergil, "and I am not yet finished. For one day, Favorita met her knight. I say she met him, but in fact she had known him for many years, as he lived not far away and had made his intentions toward her quite clear on a number of occasions. She had always insisted on these occasions that although he was nominally a knight and possessed of many admirable qualities, he lacked certain traits that she found desirable in a suitor. This frustrated knight spent many years learning to joust, swordfight and cover puddles with his cape, as well as mastering other chivalrous skills, but still she would not relent. When pressed on the specific qualities he lacked, she finally responded that her knight would have to prove himself by undertaking a long and arduous quest to vanquish evil in the land of Dis. Saddened at this delay in their courtship but heartened to have a firm plan of action, the knight set off on a quest to prove himself to his beloved. But only a month after setting out on his quest, the knight was waylaid by goblins and never returned, so poor Favorita was left to pine for him for the rest of her life."

"Her suffering must have been immense," said Handri. "Perhaps, for her, being killed by goblins was a mercy."

Vergil sighed heavily. "I hope not everyone these days is as ignorant of the principles of chivalry as you are, Handri, or the world is in sorry shape indeed. Do you not see? There is no greater destiny for a woman than to spend her entire life pining for her one true love, who will never return. And she was robbed of that life of sublime sorrow by these foul sub-humanoids!"

"I think there is something to what you say," said Handri.

"Really?" said Vergil.

"Yes," said Handri, nodding. "I think I must be a complete imbecile regarding the principles of chivalry, because that makes no sense to me whatsoever."

"Good!" exclaimed Vergil. "Accepting your ignorance is the first step toward a higher awareness of the just and beautiful, which is, after all, what chivalry is all about. Stick with me, Handri, and soon you'll be seeing the beauty of sorrow and the futility of simple pleasures."

"And the black of white, no doubt," said Handri. "But how can you know for certain what became of Favorita? Surely there is not enough evidence here to conclude that she was among those murdered by goblins. For all we know, she may have been away at the time, or the raid may have occurred long after she died of natural causes."

"Either is possible," admitted Vergil. "We can at least hope that she lived many, many years, nursing her sorrow for m—er, for the knight she loved, and eventually died of a broken heart. But I fear that she was not so lucky. A century ago this area was under constant threat from goblins and sundry other monsters."

"If that is the case," said Handri, "I wonder why this knight of hers left. Maybe he was not looking for a chance to prove himself, but rather fleeing from danger."

"You know nothing of what you speak!" growled Vergil. "My goal was to… that is, the knight had hoped to receive a commission from the authorities at Avaressa to pursue the goblins on their own turf, to end the threat once and for all. I knew this knight, and he was no coward."

Handri shrugged. "Well, that may be. But it seems to me he should have stayed home."

Vergil felt a twinge in his chest. Despite his stupidity, Handri had a way of occasionally speaking the truth. Perhaps if Vergil had stayed home, he could have come to Favorita's aid, thus simultaneously saving her life and proving his worth. But it was a hundred years too late for such regrets.

"In any case," Handri went on, seeing the troubled expression on Vergil's face, "there's no danger of goblins attacking in this area anymore."

"No danger?" said Vergil skeptically. "A knight-errant must be ever-vigilant, for when the threat seems to have dissipated, that is when the danger is greatest. And while I understand that the immediate danger has subsided to some degree over the past century, you are deluding yourself if you believe that humanity is no longer in any danger from these foul and misbegotten creatures. Goblins are inherently devious creatures, and I would not put it past them to lie low for many decades in order to lull us into a false sense of security." Handri cringed again as Vergil spoke, and Vergil took this as confirmation of his thesis. He went on, "You claim there is no reason to fear goblins, but your reaction belies your words."

Handri shook his head. "It's not the goblins I'm afraid of," he said.

"Then what is it? If you are not troubled by the threat of attack by these foul, stinking, hateful vermin, then why do you recoil so when I speak of them? You see, there you go again!"

"M'lord," said Handri, "it is not the goblins that I recoil from, but your words!"

"You are afraid of mere words?" said Vergil, frowning.

"You have to understand," explained Handri. "Things have changed since you fell asleep."

"Yes, yes," said Vergil. "So you keep saying. You told me about the Battle of Brandsveid, when the armies of the Six Kingdoms defeated the Monstrous Army. Still, I find it hard to believe the threat of these monsters has completely—"

"No, you misunderstood me," said Handri, shaking his head. "The Six Kingdoms *lost* the Battle of Brandsveid."

Vergil frowned. "Then when did the human armies drive out the monsters?"

"They didn't!" cried Handri. "That's what I've been trying to tell you."

"Don't be ridiculous," Vergil said. "That would mean Dis is under Monstrous rule!"

"Well, no," said Handri, with a confused look. He didn't elaborate.

"Well, if the monsters don't rule Dis, then humans must. Come now, Handri, it's one or the other."

Handri groaned. "I wish I knew history better," he said. "I learned a little about it in school, but things got really complicated after the Battle of Brandsveid. I don't know how to explain it. Lord Brand won, and everybody expected him to take over all of Dis, but he didn't. Now things are all just kind of…muddled. Anyway, trust me, you can't go around talking about goblins like that."

"Like what?"

"That stuff you've been saying about them being, you know…."

"Foul, stinking, hateful vermin?" Vergil offered.

"Yes!" exclaimed Handri, cringing again. "You can't say stuff like that!"

"But they are," said Vergil.

"Just stop," Handri pleaded. "Please. At least until we talk to Lord Balphry. He can explain all this stuff better than I can."

Vergil shrugged. "I'll refrain from speaking ill of goblins for now," he said, "although I fail to see what harm it does to speak the truth of their kind. If I were you, I'd be less concerned about my words and more concerned about the possibility of being waylaid in our tracks by the stinking hordes of filthy goblin scum who... I'm doing it again, aren't I?"

"Yes," said Handri, still wincing.

"All right," said Vergil. "Not another word of goblins, then. Unless we are attacked, in which case I cannot promise my language will remain entirely civil."

"Understood," said Handri, getting to his feet. "Shall we continue?"

Vergil nodded wearily, willing himself to stand up despite his creaky, sore joints. They got back on their bicycles and continued their ride.

As it turned out, Handri appeared to be correct in his assessment of the goblin threat; they encountered no one on their journey but a few workers tilling fields, and these men took no interest in a pair of travelers on bicycles. Vergil and Handri reached the estate of Lord Balphry just before dusk, riding their bicycles right up to the front porch. Handri laid his bicycle down and walked up to the door while Vergil, exhausted, pulled up behind him. Vergil was staggering toward the door as it opened and a short, broad-shouldered creature with greenish-brown skin and prominent, pointy ears opened the door.

"Back, Handri!" cried Vergil, drawing the sword from the scabbard on his back. "Lord Balphry's estate has been compromised!" The tiredness instantly left his body as the anticipation of battle came over him. He pushed Handri aside and charged at the goblin, who yelped and ran further inside. Vergil pursued him without pause.

Handri yelled something after him, but Vergil was too intent on his quarry to pay much attention. He chased the goblin through the foyer and into the drawing room, swinging his sword in front of him. "I've got this one, Handri!" he yelled. "Go around back and see if there are any others!"

Vergil pursued the goblin from room to room, gradually gaining on him. The creature appeared unarmed and was having trouble running, as he was wearing some sort of very formal-looking uniform that restricted his movements. It was a strange and very impractical costume for a goblin raider; Vergil wondered if the goblin was some sort of witch doctor or shaman. Goblins were generally too stupid to be schooled in the arcane arts, but goblin sorcerers were not unheard of. That would also explain why the brute was unarmed.

As the goblin led him through the vast house, Vergil's strength began to flag. He gasped for breath, and sweat poured down his brow. He wouldn't be able to keep this up much longer, but he was afraid that if he paused a moment in his pursuit, the goblin sorcerer would seize upon the opportunity to cast a spell. Probably not a very powerful spell—he might turn Vergil's sword into a halibut or release a swarm of gnats to distract him—but it would be enough for him to escape, and Vergil couldn't allow that. If this goblin was one of the leaders of an advance force to invade Avaress, he might have valuable information about the attack. The trick would be to subdue him without killing him.

Fortunately, the goblin made the mistake of running through the kitchen into the pantry, from which there was no escape. The goblin did his best to hide behind a sack of flour, but Vergil saw the cowardly creature's ears peeking out above it. They were shaking with fear.

"Step out where I can see you, brute!" Vergil commanded. "Keep your mouth shut and your hands in plain view. Rusty though this sword is, I prefer it to a halibut!"

The goblin raised its hands and stepped slowly into view. "P-p-please, sir," it said. "I'm just the—"

"No spells!" shouted Vergil. "Keep your mouth shut!" Vergil was now quaking himself—not with fear, but with exhaustion. It was all he could do to maintain his threatening demeanor. If the goblin decided to fight, there was little Vergil could do about it. He was about to fall over. Sweat was pouring into his eyes, but he could see the blurry figure of the goblin moving hesitantly toward him.

"Back!" he tried to shout, but it came out as a barely comprehensible wheeze. The goblin continued to move closer. Vergil's vision began to go dark and his knees buckled.

Before he hit the ground, someone grabbed him around the middle, breaking his fall. The sword fell from his hand and he sank to the floor of the pantry.

"Stop... him," Vergil murmured, half in a daze. "Sword... halibut..." The goblin approaching him was the last thing Vergil saw before his vision went dark.

Four

Vergil regained consciousness, lying on a couch in what he recognized as Lord Balphry's drawing room. The strangely well-dressed goblin he'd chased into the pantry was standing over him, regarding him suspiciously. It backed away as Vergil tried to sit up, but it needn't have worried: Vergil was in no condition to fight. He swooned and nearly passed out again.

"Goblins... taking over..." he murmured.

"Don't be ridiculous," said a familiar-sounding voice behind him. A tall man in a fine silk suit strode into the room. Burly and bald-headed, he was nearly the spitting image of Vergil's old liege, Mallech. Vergil nearly cried out in delight at the sight of the man, but caught himself. This was not Mallech, but rather Mallech's great-grandson, the current Lord Balphry, named Marko. "Wimbers is my butler," said Marko. "He's about as much threat to you as a dead pigeon."

"Dead pigeons have all sorts of germs," said Handri. Vergil looked over to see him sitting in a chair across the room. Marko turned to glare at Handri—a look Vergil had seen on the face of Marko's great-grandfather many times. "I'm just saying, you should wash your hands," Handri grumbled.

Marko turned back to Vergil. "But of course I understand that things were different in your time, and you're still adjusting. I think we can put this matter behind us if you can avoid attacking any more of my household servants." He took another step forward and held out his hand. "Lord Balphry," he said, "although you may call me Marko. It's an honor to meet you, Vergil."

Vergil slowly sat up, still regarding the goblin. He forced himself to meet Marko's gaze and shook his hand. "The honor is mine," he said, with feigned enthusiasm. "I knew your great-grandfather well. You resemble him more than a little."

Marko smiled. "A high compliment indeed," he said, with a glance to a portrait on the wall behind him. It was a painting of Mallech in full goblin-fighting regalia. Vergil remembered when Mallech had it commissioned, only a few months before Vergil left on his chivalrous quest.

Vergil returned his gaze to the goblin, who was still silently watching him. "Your great-grandfather would be appalled to know that you have let goblins into his home," Vergil said.

Marko frowned. "A lot has changed since my great-grandfather's day," he said, "as you are no doubt learning." He glanced at Wimbers the butler, who stood silently by. "But we can talk more about that later. You look exhausted. And you must be famished. I'll have Wimbers get you some food and see you to your accommodations."

Vergil looked suspiciously at Wimbers again, and Wimbers glared back at him. Vergil wasn't keen on the idea of being served dinner by a goblin, particularly one he had just tried to eviscerate, but he supposed he didn't have much choice. He also wanted to bring up the condition of his estate before he relied too heavily on Mallech's benevolence, but he found that he didn't have the strength to protest. He would have to bring up the matter tomorrow—assuming Wimbers didn't poison him or kill him in his sleep.

"We thank you for your kindness, sir," said Handri, breaking the awkward silence.

Mallech nodded and excused himself, explaining that he had some business to attend to.

"This way," said Wimbers curtly, indicating that they should follow him.

Handri helped Vergil to his feet and they reluctantly followed Wimbers into the dining room. They sat at the table and Wimbers disappeared into the kitchen, appearing a few minutes later with some bread, soup and beer. Vergil's training in chivalry, as comprehensive as it was, had not given him the ability to identify poisoned food, and he was so hungry that he may have eaten it even if he knew it might be his last meal. Wimbers left without a word and they ate in silence. At some point Vergil must have been escorted (carried?) to one of the bedrooms, because he awoke in a comfortable bed some time later feeling remarkably refreshed. The sunlight streaming through the window told him it was mid-morning. He got up and walked downstairs, finding Handri eating breakfast with Marko. Wimbers the goblin seemed to be absent, for now.

"Good morning, Vergil!" cried Marko. "You are looking much better this morning. Last night you looked like you were about to collapse."

"Old age will do that to you," said Vergil, taking a seat at the table.

Marko nodded. "It must be quite a shock to you, awaking as an old man—and with so much changed in the world."

"Indeed," said Vergil, eyeing the food on table. "In fact, I had hoped to speak with you about some of those changes." Vergil was doing his best to remain tactful, but the contrast between Marko's huge, well-maintained and luxurious estate and Vergil's own dilapidated home hadn't escaped his attention.

"Oh?" said Marko. "What's troubling you, Vergil? Handri was just explaining to me your history with goblins. Given your experiences, I suppose I can't blame you for being a bit prejudiced. But of course the world has changed while you slept, and the sooner you can accept that fact, the better. We can't have you running around trying to kill every goblin you see."

"So I've been told," said Vergil. Wimbers had come into the room to refill water glasses, and Vergil eyed him suspiciously. "And while I accept that some things have indeed changed, I wonder if you haven't been deceived by superficial appearances. A snake in a fur coat is still a snake." He was looking coldly at Wimbers as he said this, and Wimbers returned his glare. When he finished filling the glasses, he left the room without a word.

"I'm not sure how a snake could wear a fur coat," said Handri, stabbing a sausage with his fork. "It seems like it would slip right off."

"Look," said Marko, ignoring Handri. "I can see why the integration of goblins into human society would bother you. To be honest, some days it bothers *me*. But it's just the way things are. You can't find a qualified human who is willing to work as hard as my goblin servants for the pay."

"*Servants?*" asked Vergil, stunned. "You mean there are others?"

"Of course," said Marko. "My driver, my cook, the maids, the gardeners, the stable workers… they're all goblins. These old estates don't make money the way they used to, you know. I'm only able to keep this place going because of the low cost of goblin labor and my income from other investments."

"So other noblemen employ goblins as well?" Vergil asked.

"Nearly all of them," said Marko. "Particularly those who still maintain country estates such as this one. Those living in the cities have less need, but even they tend to rely on goblin valets and secretaries."

"Secretaries!" cried Vergil. "You're saying goblins can read and write?"

"Not all of them, certainly," said Marko, "but they can be trained. Many goblins are actually quite clever."

Vergil shook his head, hardly believing what he was hearing. "I suppose I should be thankful you haven't any trolls or ogres in your employ," he said.

"Goodness, no!" exclaimed Marko. "Nobody hires ogres for household help. Do you have any idea how much they *eat?* No, if you want to see an ogre at work, you'll have to head down to the quarry, where they've got several of them breaking rocks. Oh, and I hear they've got some working on the new railroad to Blinsk. Trolls are even stronger, but tend not to be very energetic workers, so they're employed mostly as bridge attendants."

Vergil gaped at him in horror. "So it's true," he said. "The monsters really *did* win. After all the hard-won gains of the past centuries, you fools have allowed the monsters to take complete control of human society!"

Marko laughed, then caught himself as he saw Vergil's face turning red with anger. "Humblest apologies, dear Vergil," he said. "I don't mean to make fun of you, but you've completely misunderstood the situation. That is, it's true that the human armies lost the Battle of Brandsveid. The monsters beat us, fair and square. And after the defeat of the Six Kingdoms, Lord Brand could easily have sent his legions into our cities to raid and plunder as he saw fit, but he did not. For it turned out that, as hard as it is to believe, Lord Brand was not interested in ruling Dis, but rather in working with the other kings to create a better Dis for both humans and monsters. And although I know you are accustomed to thinking of goblins and ogres as inherently rapacious and violent creatures bent on destruction, the fact is that most monsters simply want to be left alone, and to have a chance at earning a decent living."

"Surely you cannot be so naïve," said Vergil, staring at Marko. "This is all a trick to lull humanity into complacency! When the time is right, the monsters will rise up to subjugate you, and when that happens, you will wish that Lord Brand had crushed you quickly!"

Marko sighed and nodded. "Yes, there are still a few who believe that, although their numbers dwindle every year that the long-prophesied uprising doesn't occur."

"Maybe if you used tape," said Handri.

Marko and Vergil turned to stare at him.

"To keep the fur coat on," Handri explained.

"As I was saying," Marko went on, "Lord Brand met many times with the other six kings of Dis, and eventually they set down some rules liberalizing trade and allowing recognition of the basic rights of all humanoid creatures."

"I find that hard to believe," said Vergil. "The nobles of my day were filled with a righteous hatred for all monsters."

"Yes, and that hatred was difficult to overcome. But not even the most deep-seated prejudice can outmatch the force of human greed. The world changed in more ways than one while you were asleep, and much of that change was brought about by that very same substance that was responsible for your predicament."

"Zelaznium," said Vergil. "Yes, Handri has spoken of it, although to be honest, I'm never certain how seriously to take him."

Handri took no notice of this comment, evidently still preoccupied with the problem of keeping the snake in its fur coat.

"The discovery of zelaznium was the impetus for the invention of many artifacts that would have seemed magical during your lifetime," said Marko. "Devices that could be used to communicate for hundreds of miles, for example, or to actually see broken bones *inside* a person's body."

Vergil nodded slowly, taking this in. So Handri hadn't been exaggerating after all.

"These innovations promised vast wealth—not to mention strategic advantage—to those who could exploit them, but the secrets of how to mine, refine, and use zelaznium were all held by Brand."

"So he forced the Kingdoms of man to take in these monsters in exchange for these artifacts," said Vergil.

"'Forced' isn't the word I would use," said Marko. "But yes, he made it difficult for the rulers of the Six Kingdoms not to accept his terms."

"Thus making it possible for his agents to infiltrate all the kingdoms."

"Again," said Marko, "there are some who still believe that was Brand's intention, but most have come to accept that Brand was simply doing his best to deal with the surplus monster population in Brandsveid. He put many goblins and other monsters to work in his factories and mines, but he simply didn't have enough work for them all. So the Six Kingdoms opened their borders to allow the monsters in. This caused a fair amount of social unrest at first, but mostly people—and monsters—have adapted. I understand the situation is distasteful to you; I have mixed feelings about it myself. But we play the hand we are dealt."

"Well, I'm not sure I'll ever be able to accept that monsters are part of human society," said Vergil. "It seems wrong to me on a very fundamental level. But frankly that is not actually my chief concern at present."

"No?" asked Marko. "Then what is troubling you?"

"The condition of my estate," said Vergil. "I understand that the care of my estate passed to your family during my... slumber, and while I appreciate your seeing to it that Handri remained employed and the house remained relatively intact, I must say that I am a bit dismayed at the state of the place."

"I can sympathize with your concerns," said Marko, "but these country estates don't make money like they used to."

"Handri keeps saying the same thing!" cried Vergil in exasperation, glancing at Handri, who was nodding in agreement. "But I don't understand what it means!"

"It's difficult to explain," said Marko. "Honestly, I'm not sure I fully understand it myself. But the economy has been vastly transformed because of technological advances, the increase in trade between the kingdoms, and the influx of cheap monster labor. The end result has been a movement toward production of goods in the cities, and a decline in small farms and self-sufficient estates such as yours."

"Even so," said Vergil, "my family held interests in many profitable ventures throughout the kingdom of Avaress. I find it hard to believe that these ventures don't provide enough revenue to see to the upkeep of my estate."

"Yes, well," said Marko, suddenly seeming a bit uncomfortable. "A lot of decisions were made before my time, and I couldn't give you precise details as to the makeup of your current portfolio."

"But you have records, yes?" said Vergil. "The paperwork is in order?"

Marko frowned. "Are you sure you want to talk about this now, Vergil? You seem to be getting rather worked up, and I'm concerned it may not be good for your health."

"I am quite well," said Vergil coldly. "I would like to set up a time to review the affairs of my estate. If you are not familiar with the matter yourself, perhaps you have a goblin I could talk to?"

Marko returned Vergil's cold stare. "Of course I'm familiar with the finances," he said. "It's just... well, as you can understand, we had no idea when you would wake up, if ever. It's been over a hundred years, so there has been some... I suppose you could call it commingling of funds..."

"What are you saying?" demanded Vergil. "Can I get access to my money or not?"

"You absolutely can and will," said Marko. "But it may take a little time to sort it all out."

"How long?"

Handri, having picked up on the tension in the conversation, was now watching Marko intently. Wimbers had entered the room again, apparently to check on the food, and he too was watching Marko. Marko looked very nervous.

Suddenly he stood up. "It's a beautiful day!" he exclaimed. "Would you like to go for a walk, Vergil?"

Vergil remained seated. "I would like to finish our discussion," he said flatly.

"We will," said Marko. "I just thought it would be nice to get some fresh air while we talk. Just the two of us."

Vergil glanced at Handri and Wimbers, shrugged and stood up. "That suits me fine," he said.

Marko left the room and Vergil followed. They proceeded outside, taking a winding path that led through the large ornamental garden behind the house. Once again, Vergil noted the contrast between the overgrown, weed-infested state of his own property and Lord Balphry's immaculately manicured grounds. It seemed there was no shortage of income when it came to seeing after Marko's own needs. Still, Vergil had to admit the mid-morning sunshine and slight breeze were quite pleasant. He had recovered from his bicycle ride and yesterday's excitement, and although he still didn't feel like his old self, much of his strength seemed to have returned. Walking in the garden was so pleasant, in fact, that it required considerable effort to maintain his irritation at Marko.

"You can, of course, stay here while the repairs on your estate are being conducted," Marko was saying. "If you decide to go ahead with the repairs, that is. You may find that your resources are better spent elsewhere. Someone your age… well, it might make more sense to find a nice house in the city. I can take care of all the details."

"I do not need you to take care of anything," said Vergil. "I merely want to see the ledgers for my finances. I will make my own decisions once I have the requisite information."

"Of course," said Marko. "I wouldn't dream of usurping your authority in the matter. It's just…" He glanced nervously over his shoulder toward the house.

"What?" asked Vergil. "What are you so worried about? Listen, I can understand if you made some decisions to your own benefit regarding my estate. You never expected me to wake up, and neither did anyone else. You did not think there was any point in spending money maintaining an estate that was not used. I can appreciate that. But I am awake now, and I need to know the status of my finances."

Marko sighed. "I'm afraid it's more complicated than that," he said, glancing back toward the house again. He rubbed his chin thoughtfully.

"Then tell me!" exclaimed Vergil. "It does no good to hide the truth from me. It's going to come out one way or another. Whatever transgressions you've committed, I'm certain we can come to an understanding, as befits two gentlemen of our rank."

"Ah, Vergil!" said Marko ruefully. "Would that it were only the revelation of my own foibles that I was concerned about. I'm afraid there are happenings afoot that would dwarf any creative accounting I or my forebears may have engaged in while you slept. And if I seem reticent on the matter, it is only because I am reluctant to involve you in such troubles. I tell you the truth, Vergil: although I am glad to see you up and walking around, it would have been better for you never to have awoken—or at least to have slept another hundred years, when perhaps this current darkness will have passed."

"Current darkness?" Vergil asked, furrowing his brow. "Surely you jest. Judging by the condition of your estate, your family is as wealthy as it has ever been. You live in an age of technological wonders. And if what you and Handri have been telling me is true, you no longer have any worries about goblins raiding your property or ogres waylaying you on the road. To what 'darkness' can you possibly be referring?"

"What you say is true," said Marko, a pained expression on his face. "We no longer need to fear such attacks. In fact, we live with almost no fear at all. And that, I'm afraid, may be our undoing."

Five

"I don't understand," said Vergil. "Your lack of fear may be your undoing? Do you mean to tell me that what you and Handri have been telling me about the threat of monsters is not true?"

Marko sighed and took Vergil by the arm. He leaned close to Vergil and spoke quietly. "Handri is a good man," he said. "Reliable and trustworthy. But you may have noticed he is not particularly... perceptive."

"He's a simple man, clearly," said Vergil. "What is your point?"

"Handri has only a superficial understanding of the current situation in Dis. He is not unique in this, of course. The vast majority of people see only what is right in front of them, failing to notice patterns beneath the surface. Very few men have the mental capacity and education to see what is really going on."

"I see," said Vergil, uncertainly. "And you are one of these men?"

Marko shrugged. "I catch glimpses, occasionally. But having grown up with the illusion, seeing through it requires a great deal of effort, and I often succumb to the illusion myself. Why, it has only been in the past few months that I've even become aware of the conspiracy."

"Illusion? Conspiracy? What in Grovlik's name are you talking about?" He scowled as he noticed, not far away, a pair of goblins pruning a hedge.

Marko caught his eye. "Let's go somewhere a little more private," he whispered. "There is a gazebo just over that hill where we can sit with some assurance that we will not be overheard."

Puzzled, Vergil followed Marko over the hill to the gazebo. Marko took a seat and Vergil, glad to rest his aching joints, sat across from him.

"What's this all about then?" Vergil asked. "You spoke of a conspiracy?"

"Keep your voice down," Marko said. "Even here, I am not completely certain we are safe. They have agents everywhere, as you have already intuited."

"They?" asked Vergil, matching his tone to Marko's. "You mean the goblins?"

"Goblins and other monsters," said Vergil. "Although the monsters are merely pawns, of course."

"Pawns working for whom?"

"To answer that," Marko said, "I need to make sure you understand how powerful zelaznium is. The fact that it could put you into a coma for a hundred years is the *least* remarkable of its properties."

"Yes," said Vergil impatiently. "I have heard several times now how zelaznium has transformed Dis, and how incredibly valuable it is. Why, Handri nearly sawed my leg off to get at it!"

"Did he?" asked Marko. "Well, I've heard of people doing far worse to get just a pinch of the stuff. But what I need you to understand is *why* zelaznium is so valuable. You see, zelaznium possesses particular mystical properties related to the transfer of information over long distances. The farseeing mirrors, the z-ray machines used by doctors to look inside people's bodies, the z-scopes used to pinpoint troop movements from many miles away— they all rely on zelaznium's ability to communicate visual impressions and information."

"Alright," said Vergil. "What of it?"

"So," Marko said, speaking even lower, "what if these amazing artifacts—the farseeing mirrors, z-scopes, et cetera, are just gimmicks, designed to distract us from what zelaznium can *really* do? What if there are devices that can be used to transmit information in far broader, subtler ways? What if zelaznium, in the right hands, is far more powerful than anyone in Dis imagines?"

"Speak plainly, sir," said Vergil. "Whatever the nature of this supposed conspiracy, you've gone too far to hold back now."

Marko nodded. "You are a wise man," he said. "When you spoke to me of your finances, I feared perhaps that you were no better than this new breed of 'knights' who talks of quests and chivalry and justice, but is in the end just another penny-pinching businessman. I see now, though, that you truly are one of the few knights worthy of the name, possessed of both wisdom and courage. And if I am correct in my suspicions, you will need every bit of both of these traits. I hope your training in the ways of chivalry does not fail you."

"I find myself in the body of an old man," said Vergil, "tired and frail. But I am a knight above all. Name this evil, and I shall see it vanquished or die in the attempt."

"I am glad to hear you say that," said Marko, "although of course I hope such a sacrifice is not necessary. The truth is, you are in essence a foreigner to this land, and as such you are able to see with a clarity that eludes those of us who have grown up here. When you spoke of the monstrous threat earlier, I attempted to silence you not because you were mistaken, but because I suspect you were dangerously close to the truth. You were quite right to be worried about a monstrous uprising. These foul creatures have infiltrated every aspect of human society. They control the means of production and the flow of information. The only consolation we humans have is that the monsters are scattered and unable to coordinate their actions—but what if we are mistaken about that as well? What if these monsters are secretly in contact with each other, perhaps using some zelaznium-based technology of which humans are unaware?"

"Even if that were true," replied Vergil, "it would do them little good unless someone is coordinating their organization. Goblins in particular are poor planners and abysmal strategists. If you truly believe such an uprising of monsters is possible, then you must also believe that somewhere there is a puppet master pulling their strings. And if the zelaznium technology comes from Brandsveid, then that would be the obvious place to look for this puppet master. Who reigns now in that accursed kingdom?"

"Your deduction is insightful, as usual," said Marko, nodding, "but that question is not so easily answered. Shortly after the Battle of Brandsveid, Lord Brand set up an arcane system of government comprised of three independent branches—legislative, judicial and executive. The legislators and president are elected by popular vote, and judges are appointed for life terms by the president. He held the presidency for only the first four years, stepping down from his official position of leadership as soon as the new system was fully in place. A new president was elected, but that president, like all who followed, can do very little without the consent of the other branches. Thus no one man can claim hegemony over the country, and in fact the current holder of the executive branch is not a man at all, but an ogre named Sharkkafi. The whole system is detailed in a written document Brand called a 'constitution,' which all government officials are required to follow.'"

"What an absurd idea," said Vergil. "How can the executive get anything done if he must get consent from these other branches of government, and all the while following a set of arbitrary written rules? No country could prosper under such a scheme. Any fool could tell you that no nation can long survive unless those of proper breeding and education are allowed free rein to rule as they see fit."

"You would be amazed at how few people still believe that," said Marko. "In fact, Brandsveid has thrived beyond anyone's expectations, despite the obvious limitations of its government. And there are many agitators within the other Six Kingdoms—both humans and monsters—who would like to see Brandsveid's 'constitutional republic' replicated elsewhere. Already the councils overseeing many cities, including Avaressa, are elected by popular vote."

"Madness!" cried Vergil. "Such a scheme goes against the natural order of things. How is it possible that Brandsveid has even survived this long?"

"Theories abound on that point," replied Marko. "Some argue that its constitutional form of government actually gives Brandsveid an advantage. Others point to the ethnic diversity of Brandsveid— the fact that it is made up of a wide variety of monstrous races, as well as humans and a smattering of the higher races. But a few of us suspect that it is something more sinister that holds that accursed country together."

"You think the constitutional government is but a false front," said Vergil. "That a despot secretly rules Brandsveid from behind the scenes." He scratched his chin thoughtfully. "Presumably the same puppet master who is secretly coordinating the monsters in preparation for the uprising against humanity."

"Precisely!" shouted Marko, then clamped his hand over his mouth, as if worried about being overheard. He glanced at the goblin workers in the distance. "You see, I was right about you, Vergil. You have the capacity to see what others do not."

"But who is this mysterious puppet master?" asked Vergil. "Who is this malevolent genius who lurks behind the mask of an unworkable political system, luring all of humanity into thinking they are safe from monsters, all for the purpose of ultimately placing all of Dis under his rule? It could hardly be one man. After all, if what you are saying is true, this conspiracy has been in the works for nearly a century."

"I have a theory," said Marko, "although I lack proof. Supposedly Lord Brand was killed in an accident in one of his factories not long after he stepped down from the presidency. But no corpse was ever recovered. And while it is not common knowledge, Brand was himself half elven. Elves have been known to live for hundreds of years."

"You're saying..."

"I'm saying I think Brand staged his own death, to eliminate suspicion that he is still running Brandsveid. I think that nothing happens in Brandsveid without Brand's approval, and that the purpose of all these machinations is a monstrous uprising that will end with the complete subjugation of all human lands. Brand may be in hiding for now, but when he next makes an appearance, it will be too late to stop him. All of Dis will be subject to his tyrannical rule."

"But how could such a conspiracy be kept secret for so long?" Vergil asked doubtfully.

"A very perceptive question," said Marko, nodding. "That is where the mysterious properties of zelaznium come in. You see, I believe that Brand not only has the ability to communicate secretly with his monstrous pawns, but can also subtly communicate with all the *humans* in Dis."

"Communicate how?"

"I haven't been able to determine how it works exactly, but I suspect that Brand is able to subtly implant ideas into people's heads, to push them toward certain ideas and away from others. So while it should be perfectly clear to any intelligent human that these monsters are planning a revolt, most people remain blind to the fact because of Brand's pernicious mental suggestions. Thus the vast majority of human beings go blithely about their business, unaware of what is right in front of their eyes. When the uprising comes, it will take them completely by surprise. And to my shame, I was one of those people, at least until very recently. I would have remained so if I hadn't happened to overhear a group of goblins speaking in hushed tones about their plans. I was unable to ascertain any details, but I gathered from what I did hear that the time of the uprising is close at hand. And even though there was no mistaking their intentions, my first impulse was to dismiss my concerns as baseless paranoia—undoubtedly the result of Brand's subtle suggestions working their insidious magic in my mind. I suspect it was only my superior breeding and education that allowed me, in this one instance, to see through the illusion."

"But now that you know the truth, you should have no trouble seeing things as they really are. And you can rally like-minded noblemen to the cause."

Marko sighed. "Would that it were so, Vergil. Sadly, I have been subjected to Brand's conditioning since birth, as have all my peers in the aristocracy. It requires incredible effort for me to even keep the impending revolt at the forefront of my mind. Doubts and distractions beset me constantly—obviously the result of Brand's continuing broadcasts of disinformation. I am, for obvious reasons, afraid to write down any of my conclusions, so I must perennially remind myself of the urgency of the situation. Even so, I had nearly managed to put it completely out of my mind until just now. It took your assault on Wimbers to remind me of the threat we faced, and if it seems as if I'm making this all up as I go along, it is only because it requires a tremendous effort to maintain my awareness of the conspiracy. And despite my best efforts, I'm afraid I will soon relapse into apathy."

"If what you say is true," said Vergil, "then would I not be subject to this pernicious propaganda as well? I am unaware of any suggestive process working on my mind."

"Are you certain?" asked Marko. "You have not begun to have doubts about the dangers of the monsters in our midst?"

Vergil frowned. "Well, yes," he said, "but that was largely due to your attempts to convince me there was no danger."

Marko chuckled bitterly. "As much as I would like to take credit for your change in attitude, I'm afraid I am not that persuasive—and I would wager that you, as a knight of good breeding and thorough training in the ways of chivalry, are not ordinarily so easily shaken in your beliefs."

Vergil gave the matter some thought, and realized that Marko was right: he had been awfully quick to accept the notion that the monsters were no threat. "What is the point of telling me this, then?" Vergil asked. "For if I am unable to resist Brand's suggestions, then soon I too will succumb to the illusion."

"You must not give up hope," said Marko. "You lived forty years without Brand's suggestions poisoning your brain, and you grew up in a time when the threat of goblins and other monsters was very real. Most humans alive today have never known the horror of a goblin raid. You must use your memories and your strength of will as a Knight of the Order of the Unyielding Badger to fight back against Brand's lies! Your eyes will tell you that the monsters you see are completely innocuous, but you must not believe them. Do not give up. Whatever you do, fight! You are the only chance we have to rally any defense against the monsters before it's too late!"

"But what can I do?" Vergil said. "I am only one man, weakened by age and out of my element."

"Don't you see, Vergil?" Marko said with a grim smile. "That is also your strength! You alone can see things as they are, and no one will suspect you are a threat. Brand's plan to lull humans into complacency has worked so well that he has undoubtedly grown overconfident. I believe that someone such as yourself—clear of mind and pure of heart—will be able to identify signs of the conspiracy and trace it back to Brand himself, like a gardener following a weed to its root. You must destroy that root, Vergil. Kill Brand and stop this uprising before it's too late!"

"I wouldn't even know where to begin," Vergil protested.

"Follow your instincts," said Marko. "The city of Avaressa is a hotbed of monstrous conspiracy. If you go there and spend some time poking around, I have no doubt you'll find evidence of it. I have an apartment there where you can stay while you investigate. Handri has been in the city enough times to know his way around; take him with you as a guide."

Vergil nodded slowly, considering the matter. The more he thought about it, the more Marko's words made sense. Monsters were still monsters, even a century after Vergil's encounter with the goblins. They were greedy, cruel, spiteful, destructive creatures, and the mere passage of time could not change that fact. If goblins and ogres appeared to be living in harmony with human beings, it was because their rapacious instincts were being held in check by some coordinating power, for an even more malevolent purpose. And only Vergil could put a stop to it.

"But if Handri goes with me," he said, "then I will have to tell him about my quest to stop Brand."

"I understand why you would be tempted to do so," replied Marko, "but I would recommend against it. As you have noted, Handri is a weak-minded individual who sees only superficial appearances. He is a good man, but when such a person is forced to face the fact that his perception of reality is a lie, he will tend to react badly. Most likely he will simply refuse to believe it, and may attempt to convince you that *you* are the delusional one. I have no doubt in your ability to resist those efforts, but if you persist in your disagreement I fear that Handri may attempt to enlist others to aid him in persuading you, and that increases the likelihood that the monsters will learn of your quest before you have had a chance to work out your strategy to root out the conspiracy."

"Then I have no allies except for you?" Vergil asked, somewhat dismayed.

"I'm afraid it's worse than that," said Marko. "For I must do my best to keep up appearances, and of course Brand's diabolical suggestions will continue to work their evil on my mind. After you are gone for a few days, I may forget about the monstrous threat completely, despite my best efforts. Why, I can feel my concern fading even now. In fact, if you return here, you may very well find that I deny ever having spoken to you about this matter."

"Surely you would not do such a thing," said Vergil.

"Not intentionally," said Marko, "but the human mind is a tricky beast, and Brand is a master of manipulation. I cannot give you any assurances of what I will do if you speak to me again. Grovlik forbid, I may even turn you over to the monsters myself!"

Vergil nodded gravely, realizing the seriousness of what Marko was saying. The quest to defeat Lord Brand was his and his alone. The events that he had seen as evidence of capricious fate—his falling into a coma and then being reawakened a hundred years later—were in fact the working of some divine force, putting him in place to defeat this unprecedented evil that now loomed over the land of Dis. It was clearly this force that was represented by the horrible amorphous monster of his dreams. His quest to vanquish evil had not been stymied by his slumber after all: he had simply been put on ice until he was needed, like a champion fighter summoned from the bench when only he could save the day.

"You are a good man, Lord Balphry," said Vergil. "I see now that I was brought back into the land of the waking for just the purpose that you describe. And by Grovlik, I shall not fail. Lord Brand's wicked machinations will be defeated. Handri and I will depart on our quest shortly after lunch!"

"Excellent," said Marko. "I'll have Wimbers put the soup on now, so you can be on your way as soon as possible. And remember, don't come back here. In fact, it's probably best if you never speak to me again. About this or anything else. Don't worry about your finances or your estate. You can trust me to take care of those matters while you're gone."

"Understood," said Vergil solemnly. "I won't let you down, Lord Balphry."

Marko smiled. "I knew you wouldn't."

Six

As promised, Vergil and Handri set out immediately after lunch, hopping on their bicycles and getting on the road that would take them to the city of Avaressa to the south. Vergil had suggested borrowing a carriage and a couple of Marko's horses, but Marko insisted that bicycles were more practical transportation in town. Handri was a bit puzzled as to why they were leaving so soon, and why they were going to Avaressa rather than returning to Vergil's estate, but Vergil explained that they would be staying in the city while Marko saw to the necessary repairs.

"Then you worked everything out with Lord Balphry?" asked Handri. "I got the impression you suspected he had mismanaged your finances."

"Nonsense," said Vergil. "What you witnessed was a mere gentlemen's disagreement. Everything is perfectly in order."

"That is good to hear," said Handri. "I take it that Marko has committed to fully renovating your estate, then? How soon do you expect we'll be able to return? And will you be able to hire a full complement of servants to maintain the place? I've done what I can, but that place requires more work than I can manage on my own, and it would be a shame to see it fall into disrepair again."

"You need not worry about such things, Handri," said Vergil. "It is all being taken care of."

"And you don't think I should return to the estate to oversee things? I am, of course, at your disposal, but I don't see what good I'll do you during your stay in the city."

"You will not be needed at the estate," said Vergil. "I have some business to attend to in the city, and if things have changed as much as you have indicated, I shall require a guide. There will be no more talk of returning to the estate until my business is finished."

"Do you plan to tell me the nature of this business?" Handri said. "I ask because otherwise it might be difficult for me to determine when it is finished."

"Let me worry about that," said Vergil. "Now cease with these impertinent questions."

Handri pouted but asked no more questions. Eventually Vergil tired of his sulking and decided to try to lighten his spirits by asking him questions about his childhood. He learned that Handri was the youngest of five children; his father raised sheep on a ranch south of Avaressa. Handri's anecdotes painted a picture of an incredibly dull childhood, but it made the man happy to talk about his youth, and it afforded Vergil some insight into what it was like to have grown up in this strange world into which he had been thrown. Vergil realized after the fifth stultifying anecdote that the dullness was itself remarkable: Handri had never known what it was like to live in constant fear of monsters.

"I envy you, Handri," he interjected when he felt he couldn't take another story that revolved around sheep. "I can only imagine what it was like to experience a childhood devoid of monsters intent on your dismemberment."

"Was it really that bad?" asked Handri.

"Listen to me, Handri," said Vergil. "My best friend when I was a child was a boy named Alvys. Alvys' father owned a parcel of land that he'd never been able to farm because it was littered with boulders. But as luck would have it, one day a troll wandered into this field and fell asleep. While the creature slept, Alvys' father sank a steel post in the ground and attached a long chain to it. At the other end of the chain was a manacle, which he clamped around the troll's ankle. It was Alvys' father's intention to coax the troll into ridding his land of boulders. And do you know how he proposed to do this?"

"I couldn't begin to guess," said Handri. "Perhaps he bribed the troll with food?"

"No, dear Handri," said Vergil. "He informed us of a wonderful new game that he had invented, which he called 'trolling.' The goal of the game was to see which of us—Alvys or I—could get closer to the troll without being crushed by a boulder. No need to look so horrified, Handri. To be honest, it was great fun while it lasted. We would 'troll' for hours, dodging and weaving as the troll hurled rocks at us. Eventually, toward the end of the day, the troll would collapse from exhaustion and Alvys' father would move the post a hundred feet or so down the field. In this way, we—I say we, although of course the troll did the bulk of the work—cleared twenty acres over the course of three weeks. We'd have cleared the remaining twenty as well if Alvys hadn't stepped in a gopher hole at the wrong moment. The boulder that landed on him is still there, as far as I know. His father wrote 'Here lies Alvys' on it, and that was that."

"He didn't have the heart to continue clearing the land, I take it?"

"What?" asked Vergil. "Oh. No, it turned out he was never really interested in farming the land. He just didn't care for Alvys very much. He probably didn't care for me either, now that I think about it."

Handri stared at him in horror.

"You see," said Vergil, "it was a different time."

"So I gather," said Handri. "It is true, I have never known such dangers. My greatest fear growing up was the golem."

"The what?" asked Vergil.

"Oh, you'll think it's silly," said Handri. "I suppose, not having any fiends to be afraid of, we had to create them. My mother used to warn my brothers and me that if we didn't stop fighting, a creature called a golem would come after us. The more we fought, the bigger and stronger the golem would get."

"An effective means of forestalling conflict between siblings, I would imagine."

"You imagine right," said Handri. "All the kids I knew were terrified of the golem. Nobody was sure what it looked like exactly, but I remember one time my mother described it as a giant arising out of the mud."

Vergil shuddered, and for a moment couldn't think of why. Then he realized what it was: Handri's description of the golem had reminded him of the monster in his dream that had threatened all of Dis. But that was foolishness: there were enough real monsters to worry about without concerning himself with fictitious bogeymen. He needed to focus on his mission.

They traveled the rest of the way in silence. It was about ten miles from Lord Balphry's estate to the edge of town, and as they got closer the path transformed from an unpaved track into a wide gravel road. The bumpy gravel made Vergil wish again for a carriage, but they managed to make it into town without serious incident.

Avaressa had been a medium-sized city when Vergil fell asleep, but now it was a bustling metropolis. From what little information Vergil was able to extract from Handri, Vergil deduced that the growth was due primarily to two factors: (1) the lessening threat from goblins and other monsters pouring over the border from Brandsveid; and (2) the growth of the importance of the railroad in shipping goods from one end of Dis to another. Avaressa was evidently a major hub for the transport of raw materials to Brandsveid and the shipping of various finished products from Brandsveid to the rest of Dis. As with most subjects, Handri's knowledge of industry and economics was spotty and suspect, but Vergil gathered that most finished goods in Dis were now produced in centralized "factories" that employed dozens or even hundreds of workers. Clothing, furniture, pottery, even weapons—all of these things were now "mass-produced" in factories. Agriculture too was subject to this trend of consolidation and centralization: smaller farms had either folded or been absorbed into larger farming operations that had the money to invest in the latest equipment and relied on a ready supply of cheap goblin labor. This was, Vergil finally realized, why his estate and others like it were in so much financial trouble: they simply could no longer compete with the larger, more efficient operations.

Handri was content to regurgitate truisms he'd heard about how this new form of production made a wider variety of goods available to more people for lower cost, but Vergil couldn't help wondering what had happened to the skilled craftsmen who had poured their labor and their hearts into the artifacts they created. Vergil also suspected these changes were further evidence of the conspiracy Marko had warned him about: the trend toward mass production had started in Brandsveid with its zelaznium-based artifacts, but was evidently now being replicated across Dis. And what better way to set the land of Dis up for a monstrous revolution than to centralize the means of production of necessary goods and fill the factories with goblins? Lord Brand could simply give the signal to shut down the factories and all of Dis would be at his mercy.

Considering this possibility, Vergil nearly despaired. How could he, brave and wise knight though he might be, hope to forestall such a widespread and insidious conspiracy? His only chance, as Marko indicated, was to locate a tendril of the plot and trace it back to its source. It was hard to know at this point what that would actually mean in practice. Perhaps traveling deep inside Brandsveid itself to expose the conspiracy? Would exposing the conspiracy be enough, or would he actually have to kill Brand? Brand was even older than Vergil, but if it was true he was half-elven, then he would be a formidable opponent—and that was assuming Vergil could get to him.

But he was getting ahead of himself. First he needed to get settled in the apartment and then spend some time investigating the conspiracy. Once he had an idea what he was up against, he could start thinking about taking some decisive action. He just wished he knew how much time he had until Brand intended to put his plan into effect.

Vergil was relieved to find that despite having roughly doubled in size, the city of Avaressa didn't seem entirely unfamiliar. The most obvious difference was the addition of a massive train depot, around which most of the activity of the city seemed to revolve. Much of the traffic—largely people on foot, but some riding in horse-drawn carriages and a few on bicycles—seemed to be heading either toward the depot or away from it. Most of those Vergil saw were humans, but he spotted several goblins as well. The goblins were almost all on foot, and although it raised Vergil's hackles to see them walking around freely in a human city, they appeared to be unarmed and not engaged in any obvious mischief. If there were ogres or trolls around, they had the decency to remain out of sight.

By the time he and Handri reached the apartment—a small but pleasant space on the top floor of a three-story building near the center of town—Vergil was exhausted. He sent Handri out to retrieve some food, and was barely able to stay awake until he returned. After eating, he got into bed, falling asleep almost as soon as his head hit the pillow.

When he got up the next morning, he found Handri still fast asleep, his ape-like limbs sprawled across a couch in the main room of the apartment, snoring loudly enough to drown out the train whistle in the distance. Rather than wake him, Vergil spent some time investigating the apartment. It was well-appointed; other than food and clothing, it seemed to have everything they might need over the next few weeks. At this point he had no idea how long it would take to unravel the mystery of the grand conspiracy threatening Dis, or where it would ultimately take him, but this would certainly do as a base of operations for now. To his amazement, he found that the apartment had its own bathroom—with hot and cold running water. He took a long bath to soothe his aching joints and wash the dirt and grime from the road off his skin. For all the signs of the decline of civilization he had seen and heard of since he awoke, there did seem to be some improvements in this strange new world. Unfortunately, he had no choice but to put on the same dirty clothes he'd been wearing since he'd awoken. Most of his clothes had long ago been sold or eaten by moths, but Handri had managed to find a shirt and a pair of trousers in a closet of the estate that fit him. He wouldn't have been caught dead in such an outfit in his time, but Handri assured him the ensemble was more than decent, if not particularly befitting Vergil's station.

"Get up!" he barked to Handri, walking back into the room where Handri was still asleep. "We have work to do!"

"Eh?" groaned Handri, blinking in confusion. "What sort of work?"

"For starters, we need to get me some decent clothes." Marko had given him a purse of gold coins, which didn't even make in a dent in the debt Marko owed his estate, but would allow him to live in reasonable comfort for a few weeks.

After Handri had gotten up and attended to his needs, they took the stairs down to the street. "Now," said Vergil, taking a moment to look up and down the street, "find me a tailor."

"Hmm," replied Handri. "There's a department store this way. That may be our best bet."

"A department store?" asked Vergil. "I do not need a department. I need a decent suit."

"They have everything," said Handri. "Come on."

Vergil followed him down the road to the big, boxy building, which had a sign over the front door reading GANELON'S DEPARTMENT STORE. Below this was another sign that read MEN'S ACTIVEWEAR UP TO 50% OFF.

"I am not certain that activewear is what I require," said Vergil.

"They have all sorts of clothes. We should be able to find a suit for you."

Vergil reluctantly followed Handri into the building, which resembled a warehouse as much as a store. "Good heavens," said Vergil. "How can anyone find anything in such a place?"

Just then a young man in a suit appeared at his shoulder. "Hello, gentlemen," he said. "What can I help you with today? We currently have a sale on men's activewear for up to—"

"By Grovlik!" cried Vergil. "What are *those*?"

The salesman had been pointing to a stack of undershirts on a table next to him, and seemed puzzled at Vergil's outburst. "These?" he asked, holding up one of the shirts. It was a short-sleeved pullover cotton shirt—the sort one might wear under a proper shirt. But these shirts were evidently made to be seen, as they bore various slogans and images. The one the salesman was holding had a large picture of a goblin's head, surrounded by a mane of wavy black hair.

"It's him!" Vergil yelped. "The goblin from the train!"

The salesman seemed confused. "We have plenty of others, if this one isn't your style," he said.

"My *style*?" Vergil asked, appalled. "Do you have any idea who that is? It's..." But he couldn't come up with the name. "Who is it, Handri?"

The salesman shrugged and put the shirt down.

"Chiga Varra," said Handri. "Please, sir, the suits are over here."

"You have nothing to say for yourself?" Vergil demanded, glaring at the salesman.

"I'm going to go get my manager," the salesman said.

"See that you do!" Vergil snapped.

"Sir," said Handri, "we came here to get you a suit. Creating an uproar over a tee shirt is not going to help you resolve the business you came here to take care of."

"This *is* my business, Handri!" declared Vergil. "Do you not see? This is the exact same image that we saw on those train cars!"

"Yes," said Handri, "but it doesn't *mean* anything. It's just something that kids paint on walls and wear on tee shirts."

"You said yourself that this Chiga Varra was the leader of a goblin revolution," said Vergil. "And you've seen evidence that there is a conspiracy to spread the message of revolution throughout Dis!"

Handri frowned. "What does this have to do with the business you have here in town?"

"Can I help you gentlemen?" asked a woman in a dress who approached them. "I'm Marla, the manager."

"Well, Marla the manager," said Vergil, "perhaps you can explain *this*." He held up the shirt with the goblin's face on it.

"Ah," said Marla, with a nod. "I understand. You see, the sign clearly says *up to* fifty percent off. These are some of our more popular tee shirts, so the discount on them is only twenty percent."

"What?" asked Vergil. "No, I'm talking about this image! You are selling shirts with a goblin revolutionary on them!"

"Is that who that is?" said Marla, regarding the shirt. "I thought he was some kind of musician. I can't keep up with what the kids are into these days."

"You can't..." Vergil began in disbelief. "I demand to know where you got these shirts!"

"You're not going to find a better price," Marla said, frowning. "I can guarantee you that."

"Where did you get them?" Vergil demanded again.

Marla regarded him sternly and said, "If you continue to address me like that, I'm going to have to insist that you leave." Handri had put his hand on Vergil's shoulder and was pointing to a security guard armed with a short sword who was heading their direction.

"We're not leaving until you tell us where you got these shirts!" Vergil growled. He reached for the sword at his side, then cursed to himself as he remembered that Handri had persuaded him—against his better judgment—to leave it at the apartment.

"Please," Handri said apologetically, "My friend is... not well. If you could just let us know where these shirts come from, we'll be on our way."

Marla scowled at Handri, but picked up one of the shirts and held up the label for them to see. It read "Manufactured by Goblintex Ltd., Turner. 100% Cotton."

"Thank you!" said Handri, grabbing Vergil by the arm. "Vergil, let's go!" The security guard was coming up behind them, his hand on his sword hilt. Vergil reluctantly made for the exit.

"What was that all about?" asked Handri, once they were back outside. "Now we have to find someplace else to get you a suit."

"Forget the suit," said Vergil. "We need to find this Goblintex Ltd. Where is Turner?"

"It's a little town a few miles northeast of here. I didn't know there was anything there except farms."

"Well, this Goblintex place is there," said Vergil. "So that's where we're going. We need to get our bicycles."

"I don't understand what this has to do with the business you have to attend to. I thought you were meeting with people about repairs on your estate or something."

"This business is much more important than that," said Vergil. "Trust me. To the bicycles, Handri!"

Handri sighed but did not protest. They retrieved their bicycles—and Vergil's sword—from the storage room of the apartment building where they'd been stashed and made their way down the street. Handri suggested that they should at least stop for breakfast, but Vergil was having none of it. So intent on getting to Turner was he that Handri struggled to keep up.

They passed the railroad depot and the main entryway into town, then took a right at the road that would take them to the northeast towards Turner. They got there just before noon. As Handri indicated, there wasn't much to the town; they passed only a few ranches and farmhouses before coming to a large brick building next to a cascading stream. The water from the stream turned a large paddlewheel that was connected to the building. A faded sign on the front of the building read GOBLINTEX.

"A textile mill!" cried Vergil. "This is it!"

"It would appear so," said Handri. "But what are you planning to do here? You're not going to break into the place and start killing people, are you?"

"Of course not," said Vergil. "This is merely a fact-finding mission."

"I see," said Handri. "And what facts are we hoping to find, exactly? Does this have something to do with Marko cheating you out of money? Because I got the distinct impression—"

"Good grief, will you stop with that, Handri? The money situation is under control. I'm not at liberty to discuss with you the reasons for our current reconnaissance mission. Or rather, I could discuss it, but the nuances are beyond your understanding. Trust that I fervently hope that someday you will understand the importance of what we are doing."

"That would be nice," said Handri. "Particularly if I have to explain it to the authorities."

"Yes, yes," said Vergil. "Now quiet down." They were creeping up on the rear of the mill.

Vergil pressed his ear to the door, listening to the hum of activity within. Vergil was unable to identify most of the sounds, but clearly this was a hub for Brand's conspiracy. He turned the handle of the door, intending to take a quick look inside. But the interior of the building was so dark, compared to the glare of the sun outside, that he couldn't make anything out but vague movements. He heard voices and the clanking and humming of machinery.

"Wait here," he said to Handri, who nodded. Vergil slipped inside, closing the door behind him. He waited a moment for his eyes to adjust, but he could still only see vague shapes of machinery and the occasional movement of shadowy figures. He thought he heard talking, but the words were almost completely drowned out by the hum of the machines. In the distance, by the light of a small window high in the wall, he could make out a staircase that led to a catwalk. It occurred to him that if he could get up there, he might actually be able to see something.

He shuffled along the wall, being careful not to trip over anything in the dark, and then climbed up the staircase. When he got to the top, he found that he still could hardly see anything. How men could work in these conditions he couldn't fathom. It seemed like an incredibly depressing, not to mention dangerous, environment. Down the catwalk a few paces he saw a dimly lit lantern hanging from a hook on the wall, and he made his way toward it. Taking the lantern from the hook, he stoked it until it burned brightly, shielding his eyes from the glare. He held the lantern at arm's length, leaning over the railing of the catwalk to peer down at the mill floor below. The light did little to illuminate the place, but he could now at least make out hundreds of figures toiling away at various machines. As he stood there, trying to make sense of the operation, many of the figures craned their necks back to identify the source of the light. And with sudden horror Vergil noticed the faces were strangely bulbous and misshapen. These weren't men; they were goblins. No wonder the factory was so dark: goblins required almost no light to see.

Such was Vergil's visceral revulsion to goblins that he momentarily forgot himself, reeling in horror from the roiling mass of monsters below him. He didn't realize he'd dropped the lantern until it shattered far below, spilling blue flame across the wooden floor. Some of the oil spattered on goblins working nearby, setting their trousers on fire. High-pitched goblin shrieks filled the air as the little monsters panicked, running in all directions. The fire, aided by goblins who were tracking through the oil and fanning the flames with their movements, spread quickly. Soon it had enveloped a nearby machine, which appeared to be some sort of automated loom. Despite their chaotic movements, the goblins had managed to clear out of the area of the fire and were now streaming out of the exits—both the one Vergil had entered through and another in the back.

Realizing the fire was soon going to engulf the entire mill, Vergil made his way quickly across the catwalk and down the stairs. But as he neared the landing, a bank of shelves that were stacked high with bolts of cloth collapsed with a crash, blocking the bottom of the stairs. Vergil tried to climb over it, but the flames spread to the cloth, forcing him back. He considered vaulting over the railing, but by the time he'd managed to get one leg over, the fire had blocked that avenue as well. The factory floor was packed full of wood shelves, wood benches, and wood-framed machinery, and the fire was spreading faster than Vergil would have believed possible. The door he'd entered through slammed shut as the last few goblins fled outside, and Vergil was left alone inside the burgeoning inferno.

As the flames continued to rise, he ran back up the stairs to the catwalk, but this seemed to be a mistake as well. The hot air was collecting against the ceiling of the building, and the smoke burned his eyes and made it difficult to breathe. There was no escape: the fire would soon engulf the entire factory, and him along with it. He'd survived a hundred year coma only to die in a fire he'd started himself. The best he could hope for at this point was that the smoke would cause him to lose consciousness before the flames got him.

"Vergil!" cried a voice somewhere in the distance. Handri. Vergil looked down, expecting to see Handri peeking through the door down below, but there was no sign of him.

"Vergil!" cried the voice again. "This way!"

Vergil realized Handri's voice was coming not from below, but through a window on the far side of the catwalk. Vergil covered his nose with his shirt and ran to it. Smoke was pouring past him through the window, making it difficult to see, but by leaning far out the opening he could make out Handri, standing on the grass down below. Milling around a few yards farther away were a handful of goblins who watched as the building burned.

"You have to jump!" called Handri.

"Jump?" cried Vergil. "I may as well asphyxiate as die from the rupturing of my internal organs. At the very least, I will break a dozen bones, and given my current decrepitude, I will never recover. Better to die in a pyre and have it done with than to spend another hundred years bedridden!"

"You won't die!" cried Handri. "Just jump as far as you can!"

Vergil scowled, coughing and blinking away tears from his burning eyes. Between the smoke and his blurry eyes he was nearly blind, but somewhere down below he heard the sound of rushing water: the stream. That was what Handri had in mind. If he could clear the rocks on the edge of the stream and hit a deep pocket of water, he just might survive without major injury. It seemed like a longshot, but it was better than certain death. If he were severely maimed, he could always have Handri finish him off with the sword.

He climbed onto the sill, bracing himself in the opening and trying to get a sense of how far he would have to jump to hit the water. It really wasn't very far: the mill was built right up against a cascade of large rocks to benefit from the momentum of the falling water. The large paddlewheel to Vergil's left continued to turn, rotating a shaft that extended inside the building to power the various looms and other machinery inside the factory that were now engulfed in flame. If Vergil jumped from here—and could clear the rocks between the building and the stream—he would land in what looked like a fairly deep pool just above the cascade. He would then have to swim furiously to avoid being carried downstream and being dashed upon the rocks, but at this point that was the least of his worries.

"I do not think I can make it!" cried Vergil. It was difficult to judge from this distance—particularly since he could barely see—but the pool seemed to be a good ten feet from the foot of the building. The area between him and the water was filled with jagged rocks. It would have been a tough jump even in the prime of his youth, and his aged, atrophied legs weren't going to make it any easier.

"Then decide how you want to die," Handri yelled. "Burned to death or crushed on the rocks."

As much as Vergil didn't want to believe it, Handri spoke the truth. He had a choice between certain death and… near-certain death. Jumping seemed a terrible idea, but it was the best one available to him. His legs were trembling from crouching in the window opening, threatening to give out at any moment. He considered climbing back inside so he could move around a little and get the blood flowing again, but a glance back told him that was impossible. The whole place was now filled with smoke, and the heat on his backside was nearly unbearable. If he went back in there now, he'd never come back out.

"Jump!" Handri shouted. But still Vergil hesitated. A momentary breeze cleared some of the smoke in front of him and again he caught sight of the goblins congregated below. They were watching Vergil with great interest and—he thought—not a little glee. Curse the little monsters, delighting in his suffering. If he survived this, he'd run them all through.

Taking a deep breath, he tensed his legs and prepared to jump. But as he was about to release his grip on the window frame, something rumbled beneath him and the whole wall moved with a jolt that almost sent him careening to the rocks below. The building was collapsing beneath him, and had begun leaning toward the stream. He found himself gripping the window frame to keep from falling out of it.

Smoke billowed in front of him, making it impossible to see. How far had the building tilted? Was he above the stream now? If he jumped, would he land in the pool or overshoot it, striking the rocks on the far side? There was no way to know. If he didn't jump soon, though, the decision was going to be made for him: he could feel the building continue to list toward the stream. If he remained where he was, he would be trapped under the collapsing ruins—assuming he survived the impact. His only chance was to jump, hope to hit the deep water, and then swim upstream far enough to avoid the building as it fell. He jumped.

There was a sickening moment of free fall, followed by a plunge into cold water. His head went under and his feet struck a rock at the bottom with a jarring impact, but not enough to cause injury. He kicked off, propelling himself to the surface and for a panicked span of several seconds he tread water, trying to determine which direction was upstream. His eyes were still bleary from the smoke, and now water was pouring into his eyes. Ultimately it was not his vision but the rushing water itself that informed him of the correct direction: he had merely to swim against the current.

But, enervated and already out of breath from inhaling smoke, he soon realized he didn't have the strength to fight the torrential flow of the stream. Try as he might to get upstream, he was swimming in place, and the fiery form of the building continued to loom over him. If he didn't change tacks quickly, he was going to be crushed underneath it. Vergil took a deep breath and relaxed his arms, allowing himself to be swept downstream toward the rocks.

What followed was a chaotic sequence of falling, swallowing copious amounts of water, attempting to determine which way was up and gasping for air, interspersed with the occasional bashing of elbow or knee against the rocks. Vergil was convinced that at any moment one of those rocks was going to come into contact with his skull, putting an end to his struggles once and for all, but by some miracle he escaped this fate. His midsection slammed into something that seemed like a wooden post, and he momentarily clung to it to catch his breath and orient himself. He realized after a few seconds that he was clinging to part of the frame of the big paddlewheel, which had been thrown off-kilter and wedged against the rocks at the bottom of the stream. He heard the groaning of timbers above him, and the beam he was grasping shuddered and began to splinter as the weight of the building bore down on it. So much for catching his breath: if he stayed here, he would soon be crushed. He let go of the beam a moment before it split, and the flaming carcass of the factory lurched toward him again, raining fiery debris that splashed and sizzled around him. He dived underwater, allowing himself to be carried downstream until his lungs burned so badly he was forced to resurface. As he did, he heard the rest of the building crash into the stream behind him. He had survived.

The stream didn't fall as rapidly here, but the water still moved swiftly and there seemed to be no place to climb back onto the shore. Vergil was so exhausted at this point that he was convinced that despite his narrow escape, he was going to drown. He simply didn't have the strength to fight the current and haul himself up the steep rocks that lined the banks.

"Sir Vergil!" he heard Handri's voice cry. "Over here!"

Spinning around, Vergil located Handri, some distance downstream. He was holding a long branch in his hand that he presumably intended to use to help Vergil out of the water. Vergil paddled frantically toward him, managing to grab the end of the branch with the fingers of his left hand as he swept past. He clutched tightly to the branch as Handri pulled it toward him, but his arthritic fingers, further stiffened by the cold water, began to slip. He gasped as he lost his grip, readying himself for another plunge. But a firm hand gripped him around his wrist, pulling him toward the rocks. He manage to wedge the fingers of his right hand into a crevice, and with Handri's help, he hoisted himself onto the rocks. With Handri still pulling him upward, he managed to climb over the rocks onto flat, sandy ground. He lay there for a moment, panting, hardly believing he was still alive.

"I'll confess I know little of fact-finding missions," said Handri, leaning over him. "Would you say you consider this one a success?"

Vergil scowled but didn't have the energy to answer. Two figures were approaching from behind Handri. At first, Vergil took them for goblins, and he tried to struggle to his feet in case they intended to finish him off. But he breathed a sigh of relief as he saw that they were humans: two young men in leather armor, with swords at their sides.

"Thank Grovlik," Vergil gasped. "I assume you gentlemen are representatives of the local constabulary? We came upon this foul nest of goblins unawares, and barely escaped when it burned to the ground."

"Is this the guy?" one of the men said, turning his head to address someone behind him. A small figure with crossed arms and an angry expression on his face stepped into view. He nodded to the man.

"All right then," said the man, approaching Vergil as his comrade seized Handri by the arm. "You two are under arrest."

Seven

Vergil and Handri were thrown into the back of a wagon, their hands tied. Vergil protested that the situation was all a big misunderstanding, but their captors seemed disinclined to hear his side of the story. It didn't help that Handri was still clueless about Vergil's "business," and that Vergil wasn't inclined to reveal what he knew of the great conspiracy threatening Dis, and so would only speak in broad generalities about "investigating a threat." It was only when he mentioned Lord Balphry that the men's ears perked up.

"You know Lord Balphry?" one of them asked, glancing back at Vergil from the driver's bench. His partner was steering the wagon onto the road back in the direction of Avaressa.

"Of course I know Lord Balphry!" exclaimed Vergil. "I'm a knight of the Order of the Unyielding Badger. Lord Balphry is my liege. Why, he is the whole reason I—" He caught himself before he revealed too much.

"He's the reason you what?"

"Never mind," said Vergil. "I demand that you release me. What are the charges?"

"Arson," said the man. "And attempted murder."

"Murder!" cried Vergil. "That factory was a haven for foul, degenerate monsters who seek to extinguish all that is good and beautiful in the world. A quick death by incineration is far too good for their kind!" He thought for a moment, then added, "Also, it was an accident."

"Forgive me if I'm overstepping the bounds of my station," said Handri, leaning over toward Vergil, "but it might be a good idea to stop talking now."

Vergil grunted but did not reply. The two men, for their part, seemed uninterested in Vergil's tirade, apparently having concluded that he was a raving lunatic. They rode the rest of the way back to Avaressa in silence. Vergil and Handri were shuffled into a cell in a dungeon somewhere beneath the city. Sometime just before dark they were each served a bowl of something that was either porridge or wallpaper paste, which Handri lapped up. Vergil, despite having had nothing else to eat that day, found himself with little appetite.

Vergil, exhausted from the day's adventures, slept fitfully on a mattress stuffed with straw. In the morning, he awoke to the sounds of voices in the hall. "—demand that you allow me to see him," a man was saying. After a moment's confusion, Vergil realized that he recognized the voice: it was Marko, Lord Balphry himself.

"Thank Grovlik," Vergil murmured to himself. Marko knew the importance of Vergil's mission; he would see to it that he was released to continue his quest. He nudged Handri, who was still snoring next to him. "Wake up, Handri," he said. "We've got a visitor."

Marko strode into view, barely recognizable in the dim light from an overhead grate, followed by a guard. "Open it," Marko commanded, indicating the cell door. The guard hesitated for a moment, but then unlocked the door and opened it. Marko strode inside. "Leave us," he said. The guard nodded, closed the door and shuffled off down the hall.

"Very good to see you, Lord Balphry," said Vergil. "Handri and I ran into some complications during a routine fact-finding mission yesterday, and it seems that the local authorities have an exaggerated sense of—"

"Shut up, Vergil," Marko snapped. "You've made your point. Just tell me what you want."

"My point?" asked Vergil, confused. "I'm afraid I don't follow you. Listen, I understand that the incident at that factory may have led you to believe I'm being overzealous in my pursuit of..." He glanced at Handri. "...the business we recently discussed, but you must not doubt my long-term commitment to the cause. This was only a minor misstep, and as soon as Handri and I are released, we can get back to work."

"Is that a threat?" Marko asked, glaring coldly at Vergil. "Because I can see to it that you rot in here, if that's what you really want."

Vergil regarded Marko in puzzlement. "Certainly not," said Vergil. "I meant only to say that we remain in your service, and that our service is likely to be more satisfactory if we are not confined indefinitely to an underground cell."

Handri nodded, and Marko stared at them, realization slowly dawning on his face. "So," he said after some time, "you really don't know?"

"Know what?" asked Vergil.

Marko shook his head slowly. "When I heard you'd burned down that mill, I assumed you had…"

"What?"

"Never mind," said Marko. He let out a long sigh, rubbing his forehead with his hand. "Did any goblins die in the fire?"

"I don't think so," said Vergil. "They ran for the exits as soon as the fire started. Little bastards stood there and watched as the place went up in flames around me."

"And you haven't attacked anyone else? Or wrecked any other property?"

"Besides the factory?" asked Vergil. "No."

"Okay," said Marko. "Well, that's something. The good news is that I shouldn't have any trouble getting you out of here, because the owner of that factory is unlikely to press charges against you."

"I should hope not," said Vergil. "If one is going to employ goblins, one needs to be prepared for the sort of mayhem that inevitably ensues. Who is this fool, anyway?"

"That's the bad news," said Marko, with a grimace. "I see now that perhaps I should have been more accommodating when you requested a full accounting of your finances. In my defense, I don't think I could have been expected to foresee your affinity for arson."

"Hold on," said Handri. "Are you saying…."

"What I'm saying," Marko said, "is that the bulk of Vergil's portfolio is currently made up of stock in Goblintex Limited." He turned to Vergil. "You burned down your own factory, old chap, and most of your assets with it. You're penniless, Vergil."

Vergil gaped at him in horror. "This must be a joke," he said at last. "My family would never invest its fortune in a company run by goblins!"

"That's probably true," said Marko. "But when you went down for your hundred year nap, the care of your estate fell to my family. My grandfather, seeing the decline in the profitability of small farms, sold off most of your holdings and invested the returns in various business endeavors. My father sold most of those holdings and bet big on a single enterprise—a little shirt-making business down by the river run by a pair of enterprising goblins that eventually came to be called Goblintex. With his help, they were able to build that factory, which employed over two hundred goblins up until yesterday."

Vergil shook his head, taking this all in. "But... if your father believed so strongly in the prospects of Goblintex, then he must have invested some of his own money as well. Are you not also taking a great loss as a result of the fire?"

Marko smiled grimly. "Interestingly, my father saw fit only to invest *your* money in Goblintex. I couldn't speculate as to his motives."

"Really," said Vergil flatly. "You are certain that perhaps you aren't taking advantage of the ambiguity in my finances to retroactively reallocate some of my funds?"

"I'm sure I don't know what you mean," said Marko.

"You're lying!" Vergil cried. He gripped his skull in his hands and moaned. "I was a fool not to see it. You deliberately concealed my holdings from me. By Grovlik, this whole quest was probably a red herring, meant to prevent me from looking into your malfeasance."

Handri raised an eyebrow at him. "Quest?" he asked.

"And now that the factory has burned down," Vergil went on, "you're going to doctor the books to make it look like it was only *my* money that was lost. Was any of my money even invested in Goblintex? Do you even know what money is yours and what's mine anymore? Or did you just put it in one big pot to use as you saw fit, assuming that I would never wake up?"

"What a ridiculous allegation," said Marko. "The very idea that I absorbed your holdings into my own portfolio, and that at this moment some poor goblin accountant is revising all my ledgers to make it seem as if all the money that was invested in Goblintex was yours... preposterous! Regardless, I think we can all agree that it was your actions that brought about the demise of Goblintex, and therefore it is only just that you bear the brunt of the loss."

"You son-of-a-bugbear," Vergil growled, taking a step toward Marko. He trembled with rage. "I am going to—"

"You're going to *what*, old man?" snapped Marko, the burly man towering over Vergil. "You touch me, and I'll break you in half. And don't forget, this is all for your own good. It's only because you burned down your own factory that you're getting out of here. If I claim even a one percent stake in Goblintex, I could have you hanged for arson. So you can either go along with the story that Goblintex is all yours, or you can rot in here until they hang you."

Vergil's shoulders sagged as he realized it was the truth.

"And you don't lose a thing," said Handri to Marko.

"On the contrary," Marko said, turning to face him. "I had fully intended on bilking Vergil out of every penny, so I'm taking a significant loss as a result of your little stunt yesterday."

"Forgive me if I do not shed a tear for your inability to extort me as thoroughly as you had planned," Vergil muttered.

Marko shrugged. "I'll get over it." He walked to the door and summoned the guard, who opened the door for him. "Let these two out as well," said Marko.

"I'm sorry, m'lord," said the guard. "But I can't—"

"You can and you will," snapped Marko. "This was all a misunderstanding. My good friend Vergil was simply demolishing his own factory to make way for a bigger one. He's the owner of the company. I have all the paperwork at my estate."

The guard stared at Vergil, his brow furrowed. "Is that true? You burned down your own factory?"

Vergil looked to Handri, who shrugged. Vergil sighed. "So it would appear," he said.

"All part of the new capitalist system, good fellow," said Marko, with a broad smile. "Creative destruction."

"Sounds like old-fashioned stupidity to me," said the guard. "But I can't let them out unless my boss tells me to."

"Listen to me, boy," said Marko. "You know who I am, right?"

"Of course, Lord Balphry."

"Good. Then you're going to let these men go, and if your boss has a problem with it, he can talk to me. Alternatively, I can talk to your boss first, and you can get a jump on looking for a new job."

The guard swallowed hard and motioned for them to leave the cell. They made their way back to street level, where Marko's carriage waited for him.

"What do we do now?" asked Handri, as Marko climbed onto the carriage.

Marko turned and gave a shrug. "That's up to you," he said. "I've got a tenant moving into the apartment next week, but you can stay there until then. Consider it my parting gift to you." He got into the carriage, and a moment later it was gone in a clattering of hooves.

"I'm famished," Vergil announced. "Let's get some breakfast."

Handri nodded and followed as Vergil made his way down the street to an inn. They sat and ate in silence, but Vergil could see that Handri was resisting the urge to say something.

"Alright then," Vergil said irritably. "Out with it. You have some criticism regarding my behavior at the factory? Or my handling of our situation with Lord Balphry?"

"No, sir," said Handri. "In fact, I admire your single-minded pursuit of your objective."

Vergil accepted the compliment with a nod.

"The only question I have," said Handri, "is... well, what *is* your objective exactly? What was this quest you spoke of?"

Vergil sighed. "I'm afraid my enthusiasm and naiveté have been my undoing. Lord Balphry duped me, convincing me that I was humanity's only chance to resist a monstrous uprising led by Lord Brand."

Handri frowned. "Lord Brand has been dead for years," he said. "And from what I know of history, he was never particularly interested in leading any kind of monstrous uprising. He could have overrun the Six Kingdoms right after the Battle of Brandsveid if he had wanted to."

"So I gather," said Vergil. "I'm embarrassed to admit that Marko successfully played on my ego and my prejudices, blinding me to both his financial malfeasance and the absurdity of the supposed plot. The idea that goblins—" He broke off as a serving wench, a goblin who would not have been identifiable as female were it not for her garish makeup and corset, approached their table with a pitcher of beer.

"You gentlemen all right here?" she asked, peering inscrutably at Vergil. It was impossible to tell how much she had overheard. Vergil and Handri both nodded anxiously. The goblin wench shrugged and went about her business.

"And is there truly nothing you can do about Marko stealing your family's fortune?" Handri asked. "Perhaps you could hire a lawyer to fight him in court."

Vergil shook his head. "Such a course of action would be unbefitting for a knight. And probably pointless in any case. I am no expert in the law, but Lord Balphry would seem to have me over a barrel."

"Then what will we do? I could perhaps find work as a groundskeeper or street sweeper, but how will you live? Do you have any marketable skills?"

"I have a great many skills," said Vergil, "although I would not condescend to market them. A knight serves for honor, not for money."

Handri nodded, rubbing his chin thoughtfully. "And how long do you suppose your stores of honor will last you?" he asked. "Or did Lord Balphry steal that as well?"

Vergil scowled but didn't respond. He hated to admit it, but Handri had a point: if he didn't find some way to make some money soon, he was going to be reduced to begging for crumbs on the street—or starving, which might be preferable.

He was still ruminating on this when a portly, round-faced man silently approached their table and sat down. Vergil was about to object, but something in the man's earnest, intense manner made him hold off. "I apologize for the intrusion," the man said in a voice barely above a whisper, "but I couldn't help overhearing what you said about the...." He glanced furtively at the goblin wench. "About *them*."

"You mean the goblins?" asked Handri.

"Shh!" the man hissed. "Not just goblins. Ogres and trolls, too. And *sympathizers*." He said this last as if it were the worst of the four. He held out his hand to Vergil. "My name is Collamer."

Vergil reached over and cautiously shook the man's hand. "Vergil," he said. "Knight of the Order of the Unyielding Badger. This is my, ah, servant, Handri."

Collamer smiled politely at Handri, then turned back to face Vergil. "Oh, I *know* who you are. You're the reason I'm here."

"I am?" asked Vergil, confused.

"Sure," said Collamer. "I wouldn't be caught dead in a place like this otherwise. Who knows what *they're* putting in the food." He glanced again suspiciously at the goblin server. Vergil and Handri regarded their eggs and toast dubiously. "I heard you'd been thrown in the dungeon for burning down that goblin factory, and I followed you here."

"You suspect the monsters are up to no good?" asked Vergil.

"Monsters *are* no good," said Collamer.

"I thought you'd concluded there was no conspiracy?" Handri said to Vergil, a pained expression on his face.

"Conspiracy?" said Collamer. "There's no conspiracy. You gotta have a brain to conspire. Monsters are just upright animals. They breed until they spill over into human lands, taking their crime and filth with them."

"You'll get no argument from me," said Vergil. "I have seen firsthand what these foul subhumanoids are capable of. But why are you telling us this? Why did you seek me out?"

Collamer smiled a broad, gap-toothed smile. "Because," he said, "I want to offer you a job."

Eight

"A job?" Vergil asked, frowning. "I have…" He turned to Handri.

"No marketable skills," Handri said.

"Right," said Vergil. "I have no marketable skills. And if I had, I would not market them."

"You haven't heard how much this job pays," said Collamer.

"It makes no difference," said Vergil, holding up his hand. "A knight cannot be bought." He paused. "Out of curiosity, how much *does* it pay?"

"Enough to get you into a nicer apartment," replied Collamer.

Vergil scowled. "What's wrong with our apartment?"

"Oh, there's nothing *wrong* with it," said Collamer. "But I think we can find a place more befitting of your station as a knight. And if I understood you correctly, you will soon be looking for another place anyway."

"But taking the menial, undignified job which you are undoubtedly offering me will only undermine my claim to knighthood," said Vergil. "I cannot sacrifice my honor for material comfort."

"The job I offer is hardly menial," said Collamer. "You will be leading a group of honorable men in a just cause. And we'll get you a horse."

"A horse?" Vergil asked. His thoughts went to brave, loyal Penumbra, whose spirit was now undoubtedly running free in the fields surrounding the Hall of Avandoor. And then his thoughts drifted to the wobbly, undignified bicycle he had ridden from his estate—and which had almost certainly been purloined by goblins from the clearing next to the factory where he had left it. "I suppose I could deign to accept some payment for service, given that the service is sufficiently dignified. Tell me more of this operation," he said. "What will I be doing exactly?"

Collamer smiled. "I have spoken to you about the threat we face from goblins, and I know you need no convincing on that front. Like me, you are appalled by the changes that have taken hold of Dis—the encroachment of monsters and the gradual dissolution of civilized society. There are many who hold these opinions, but few have the courage to do anything about it. Our political leaders are deaf to our concerns, as they have become dependent on artifacts imported from Brandsveid and have convinced themselves that humanity as a whole benefits from the ready supply of cheap labor offered by monsters pouring over the borders. Thus it has fallen to people like me to resist."

"Resist how?" asked Handri skeptically.

"I am a local businessman," Collamer explained. "I am by no means wealthy, but I make a decent living for myself, and I am the president of a local association of other small businessmen. Most of our members share my feelings about monsters and what they have done to our once-proud city. Together I believe we have the numbers and influence to push back the monstrous horde, but...." He broke off, raising his hands in a gesture of helplessness.

"But what?" asked Vergil. "What do you lack? Equipment? Training in tactics?"

"Leadership," Collamer sighed. "As loath as I am to admit it, I'm an organizer, not a leader. I can put a plan together on paper, but I can't inspire men behind an idea. That's why we need you, Vergil. When I heard that you had awoken from your sleep, I suspected you were the man to lead our movement. And when I heard about what you did at that factory, well, I was certain of it. 'Here is a man who hates goblins as much as I do,' I thought."

"You seem to be keeping fairly close tabs on me," said Vergil.

"You're something of a celebrity," Collamer said. "Why, there's hardly anyone in Dis who hasn't heard the legend of old Vergil the knight, who inhaled a cloud of zelaznium and slept for a hundred years. Of course, not many these days believe you actually exist, and fewer still have heard that you awoke and are now walking among us. The symbolic power of you leading us… it will be like a voice from the past reminding us of how things are supposed to be."

"I am not a symbol to be carted around to inspire confidence in the troops," said Vergil.

"Of course not!" said Collamer. "You're so much more than that. As I said, these men need a leader. You're trained in the ways of chivalry, and you know more about the goblin menace than anyone. As far as I'm concerned, you're the best—the only—choice for the position. I didn't think I had a chance of actually securing you, though, until I happened to overhear you talking with your friend here about your financial troubles. I think we can come to a very satisfactory arrangement. We can find a place for your friend as well."

Handri nodded politely, though without much enthusiasm.

"What would I be leading these men to do exactly?" asked Vergil.

Out of the corner of his eye, Vergil saw the goblin server approaching again. Collamer glanced at her and leaned closer to Vergil. "Meet me at the northern gate tonight at dusk," he said. "We can talk more then." He got up and moved to the door without another word.

"What do you think that was all about?" asked Handri, when the goblin had moved past their table.

"I suppose we'll find out," said Vergil.

"You aren't actually thinking of meeting him?" said Handri.

"I don't see the harm," said Vergil. "Now finish eating. I need to wash up and get a suit."

Handri groaned, although it was unclear whether this was in anticipating the meeting with Collamer or in remembrance of their last attempt at getting Vergil a suit. But the rest of the day passed without serious incident. They returned to the apartment, slept for a few hours, got cleaned up, and then found a clothing store that had a decent suit in Vergil's size. It cost them half of the money they had left, but Vergil insisted that he couldn't be seen around town in rags anymore—particularly if he was going to be expected to live up to his celebrity. They ate dinner and then made their way to the city gate, getting there just as the sun set. A group of maybe two dozen men was already there, waiting for them. Several horses stood around, whinnying and looking bored.

"Vergil!" cried a portly silhouette Vergil recognized as Collamer. "And, uh…"

"Handri," said Handri.

"Of course. Welcome, gentlemen, to the first official field outing of the KLAMP!" Whoops and cheers went up from the group.

"KLAMP?" asked Vergil.

"Knights for the Limitation of the Advancement of Monstrous Populations," Collamer explained.

Vergil regarded the motley assortment of men and their slightly more impressive horses. "You call these men knights?" They didn't resemble any knights Vergil had ever known: they were paunchy and round-shouldered, wearing frilly clothing that was at once too luxurious and not durable enough for either riding or combat. A few of them had swords or daggers at their sides, but no helmets, and the pieces of armor they wore seemed to be more decorative than practical.

"Of course they're knights!" Collamer exclaimed. More cheers went up. Collamer leaned close to Vergil and said, "They aren't *really* knights, of course. But the name helps to reinforce the team dynamic." Vergil nodded, not having a clue what Collamer was talking about. "Men," said Collamer, turning to the group, "allow me to introduce a man who is truly a living legend, the last remaining Knight of the Order of the Unyielding Badger, Sir Vergil Parmeligo!"

More cheers and applause from the group. Several of the men climbed onto their horses, as if expecting to depart somewhere.

"I don't mean to rush things," said Collamer, "but we just received word that a throng of goblins is on its way to the city. If we don't stop them, no one will. We could really use your help, Vergil."

Vergil frowned, realizing what was going on. "This is vigilantism," he said. "This outing is not approved by any legitimate authority." Handri nodded furiously.

"Of course not," said Collamer. "I already told you the local authorities are worthless. If we're going to stem the tide of monsters pouring into human lands, we have to take matters into our own hands. You aren't frightened, are you, Vergil?"

Vergil snorted. "Where is my horse?" he asked.

"I'll get him for you," said Collamer with a smile, and trotted away.

"Sir," said Handri, "I really don't think this is a—"

"Quiet down, Handri," said Vergil. "I've made my decision. Look at this group. They'll be completely helpless without me."

Handri frowned at the group of men. One of them was trying to keep his horse from eating the straw hat of the man in front of him. Another had dropped his sword and was in the process of trying to pick it up without getting out of the saddle. Handri and Vergil winced as the man fell on his head.

"I suspect they'll be helpless either way," said Handri.

"Admittedly, it will take some time to whip them into shape," replied Vergil. "But they are well-intentioned and their mission is a worthy one. We'll turn back these goblins that threaten the city and then see what we can do about enforcing some discipline in this group."

As he spoke, Collamer approached on a horse, leading another by the reins. He slid off the saddle. "This one's yours," he said to Vergil. "And this one is for…"

"Handri," Handri said again.

"Do you have a sword for Handri?" Vergil asked.

After some negotiations with the other men, Collamer produced a short sword in a battered leather scabbard. He tried to remove it, but found it stuck in place: it had corroded so badly that it had somehow become fused with the leather. Handri took it from him but was also unable to remove it. "Well," said Vergil, "it probably doesn't have much of an edge anyway. Just try to look intimidating. Use it as a club if you have to."

Handri gave a dismayed nod, but slipped the scabbard through his belt.

"Great," said Collamer. "I'll be right behind you. Let's go stop some goblins!"

Vergil climbed into the saddle and Handri reluctantly did the same.

"We had a report the goblins were about five miles to the northeast a few minutes ago," said Collamer. "We should be able to head them off in plenty of time."

"Any idea how many?" Vergil asked.

"Our spy says maybe a hundred," replied Collamer.

"A *hundred goblins?*" cried Handri. "We can't fight off a hundred goblins!"

Collamer chuckled. "A wise man once said that creatures of weak mind cannot but bend their will to the irresistible force of a one well-schooled in the arts of chivalry."

Vergil frowned. "*I* said that."

"I know," replied Collamer. "Your squire Salivar recorded your final words."

"Then you know how that encounter ended."

"Yes, but this time you have experience on your side."

Vergil sighed. He wasn't sure how to explain that sleeping for a hundred years didn't somehow magically make him wiser or more capable of handling a hundred rabid goblins. All it had done is make him weak and tired. In fact, at this moment he wanted nothing more than to go back to the apartment and lie down to rest his aching joints. But if he did that, these courageous—if somewhat foolish and unprepared—men would be forced to face the goblin horde alone, and they would no doubt be slaughtered. Perhaps he could prevent that if he went with them, although he didn't have much hope they'd actually be able to halt the goblins' advance. No, there was nothing to do now but put on a brave face and lead these men against the goblins.

"All right, men," Vergil shouted, "Follow me!" He gave his horse a kick and she started forward. Handri maneuvered his own steed next to him, and Collamer and the others fell into line behind them. Handri didn't speak, but Vergil could tell he was afraid. Vergil felt bad for him; the man was just a caretaker with no training in combat, but Vergil couldn't dismiss him without raising doubts among the other men. The only thing this group had going for it was bravado: if they could convince the goblins they were not to be trifled with, it might be possible to scare them off without having to fight. It was a long shot, but it was the only one they had.

They rode in silence for about three miles. The sun had set and they were now riding in near-total darkness. A few of the men had thought to bring torches, and Vergil held one over his head, craning to see in the gloom ahead. The goblins would no doubt see them first, torches or no, as they could see in the dark. In any case, stealth was not their ally; they needed to appear completely unafraid of the goblins or they were doomed.

They heard the goblins before they saw them: first the creaking of wooden wheels on gravel, and then the sounds of murmurs in the darkness. Vergil could make out the shape of several wagons and many more goblins on foot, but it was impossible to judge the size of the horde. He could only assume that they had seen the torches and had decided to press on.

"Hello there!" cried Vergil, holding up his hand in a signal to the others to stop.

There were muffled sounds of talking in the distance, and then the noise of the wheels stopped. A single goblin emerged from the darkness into the glow of Vergil's torch. As it approached, Vergil saw that the goblin was female.

"Good evening," said the goblin, with a genial smile. "Apologies if our party is blocking your way. I'll have the drivers pull over to the side so you can pass. I hope that's agreeable to you." Vergil saw that she was holding something in her arms.

"Actually," said Vergil, "We seem to have reached our destination. Our band of knights plans to travel no farther tonight." He added, after a pause, "On the condition that your group halts as well."

"There is nothing here for us," said the goblin. "And nothing behind us either. We seek only to travel to the city of Avaressa, to start a new life there."

"There is no place for your kind in Avaressa," said Vergil, placing his hand on his sword. "Turn back and return from whence you came."

"We can't," said the goblin. Another young goblin ran up behind her and hid behind her legs. "Are we almost there, mama?" he asked. "I'm sleepy." Vergil realized that the female was carrying a baby in her arms.

Vergil frowned and turned to Collamer, who had come up on his left. "You didn't say they had women and children with them."

"Goblins are goblins," said Collamer, with a shrug. "Some are easier to catch than others."

Vergil shook his head. It was true that all goblins were filthy brutes, but typically only their males were warriors. Threatening females and children seemed unsportsmanlike. "Why can't you return to the place from whence you came?" he asked.

"Because you burned it down," the female said flatly.

Virgil was taken aback. "I... You worked at the shirt mill?"

"We all did," said the leader of the group. "I was the mill forewoman. Many of us slept there as well. We're still hoping the owner shows up with a plan to rebuild the place. But so far we haven't seen him, and we're running out of food. We're hoping to stay with friends and family in the city until either the mill reopens or we can find other work."

"This is ridiculous," grumbled Collamer. He glared at the goblins. "Disperse!"

The goblins stared at him, without speaking. The infant began to cry.

"Vergil, I don't feel right about this," Handri murmured.

Vergil sighed. "Allow me a moment to confer with my compatriots."

The goblin leader nodded, and Vergil brought his horse around to speak with the others. "Listen," he said. "This is not exactly what I signed on for. This is no horde of goblin invaders. It's a caravan of refugees. We are not prepared to deal with this."

"There's only one way to deal with goblins!" one of the men cried. He drew his sword and several of the others cheered.

Collamer nodded. "I don't see how the makeup of the group makes any difference. If anything, females are worse, because they breed more of the vermin."

Murmurs of agreement were heard.

"There would be no honor in such a battle," said Vergil, "and from what I've gathered of the current legal climate, I suspect an attack on non-belligerent goblins would likely land us all in prison. My companion and I already spent a night in a dungeon merely for burning down one of their factories, and only escaped on a legal technicality. I am all for dealing with the monstrous menace at the appropriate time, but I'm afraid we have no choice but to allow these goblins to pass unmolested into the city."

Disgruntled murmurs arose from the group. Someone in the back spoke the word "traitor." While Vergil was still deliberating over how to convince his overly enthusiastic band of "knights" to back down, Collamer dug his heels into his horse and drew his sword. The horse darted past Handri toward the goblins, but as it did so, Handri gave Collamer a poke in the ribs with his sword (still rusted into the scabbard), knocking him off balance. Collamer, obviously not a skilled horseman, tumbled out of the saddle and landed with a thud on the ground. The horse went a few more steps, then turned and whinnied at him as if embarrassed of its rider.

"Well done," said Vergil, genuinely impressed with Handri's quick thinking and reflexes. Handri nodded at him. "Handri and I will not permit anyone to harm these goblins. Would anyone else care to test us?"

More murmurs arose, but no one spoke up or made a move.

"Fine," said Vergil. "Then move to the side of the road so that the goblins can pass."

The men reluctantly maneuvered their mounts to the side of the road. Collamer got up, glaring at Handri. He glanced at his sword, which he had dropped when he fell.

"If you do anything with that sword other than return it to its scabbard, I'll run you through myself," said Vergil. He wouldn't have done it, but he tried to sound convincing.

Collamer grunted and retrieved the sword, replacing it in the scabbard. He took the horse's reins and led it to the side of the road.

"Much obliged for your kindness," said the goblin to Vergil.

"'Tis not kindness," said Vergil irritably. "Make no mistake: your kind has no place in human society. But this is not the time for a battle between our two races. Unlike subhumanoids, humans are capable of reason and decency, and slaughtering your party now would neither serve our interests nor reflect the gallant nature of our kind."

"Oughta kill 'em while we have the chance," one of the men grumbled behind him.

"There seems to be some disagreement among your camp regarding these vaunted human capabilities," said the goblin, "but I am gratified that there is at least one genuine human among you, and that his gallantry prevents him from engaging in wholesale murder, if not unprovoked arson."

Vergil scowled, but resisted the urge to respond in kind. "Do you have any weapons with you?"

"A few clubs and knives," said the goblin. "We had intended to turn them in at the city gate, as we understand is the custom."

Vergil nodded. He considered demanding to inspect the wagons, but wasn't sure what he'd do if the goblins refused. He'd already acknowledged his reluctance to fight; if the goblins objected to an inspection, he didn't have the will or manpower to force the issue. Better to follow the party into town and ensure as best as he could that their intentions were peaceful.

He guided his horse to the edge of the road. "You will be permitted to pass. You have my word that none of my men will attempt to interfere with your passage as long as you do not initiate hostilities." He shot a steely glance over his shoulder at the men to make sure they knew he meant it.

The goblin nodded back and disappeared with her children into the shadows. Moments later the sounds of wheels on gravel resumed, and soon several wagons, some drawn by mules and others by teams of six or eight goblins, began to roll past. From inside the wagons, he heard the voices of many more goblins, young and old, and he sighed. Was this really the gallant course of action? Or had he lost his nerve after his long slumber? He'd never even *seen* a female goblin before, to say nothing of goblin children. On some level he'd been aware that they existed—they had to, after all—but it was only male goblins in their prime years who were sent to raid towns and waylay travelers. In his mind, "goblins" meant a bloodthirsty horde of armed killers. He simply hadn't been prepared for a pathetic group of refugees. And he wasn't certain that his own guilt over burning down the mill didn't play some part in his reluctance to engage them.

When the goblin caravan had passed, Vergil and Handri followed behind them, enduring the angry stares of their companions. "Fall in line, men," Vergil said. Handri shot him an anxious glance, but Vergil ignored him. He knew what Handri was thinking, but there was no point in worrying about it: if the men decided to attack them from behind, they were defenseless.

But the journey back to Avaressa passed in uneventful silence. The guards at the gate were a bit taken aback by the sudden appearance of the refugees, but after some discussion apparently concluded they had no authority to refuse them entry. They did a cursory search of the wagons, confiscating a few crude weapons. The other "knights" watched sullenly from their horses, clearly wanted to intervene, but afraid to do so in front of the city guard.

"Let's go home, Handri," said Vergil, slipping off his horse. Handri did the same. They handed the reins to Collamer, who scowled but said nothing. Vergil and Handri walked back to their apartment. It was safe to say that they were no longer gainfully employed.

Nine

Vergil was awakened early the next morning by a banging on the apartment door. He groggily put on his pants, grabbed his sword, and ran into the main room, where Handri was standing with his ear to the door.

"Who is it?" Vergil asked. Handri shrugged.

Vergil frowned. He suspected some of the "knights" from the previous night's adventure had gotten up the courage to challenge him about his spoiling of their fun. Vergil repeated the question with more volume.

"My name is Bander," said a muffled voice through the door. "I was with the… group you met last night. I'm alone and unarmed."

Vergil and Handri shared dubious glances.

"Please," said the voice. "I need to speak to you regarding an urgent matter. It's in your interest, I promise."

"What is this urgent matter?" asked Vergil.

"I—I'm not comfortable speaking about it out here. If you let me in, I can explain everything. Please, you are in great danger."

Vergil sighed. He didn't trust this man, whoever he was, but neither did he intend to live in fear of the KLAMP. Better to face them down now and get it over with. He nodded to Handri to open the door, and Handri did do, reluctantly. A young man slipped inside, looking nervously over his shoulder. Vergil recognized him as one of the men who had hung toward the back of the group of "knights."

"Speak then, Bander," said Vergil, "if that is your real name."

"I've come to warn you," said Bander. "The authorities have been watching the KLAMP for some time now, looking for some reason to disband or arrest them. But up until last night, all the KLAMP did is talk—because frankly, at heart they are cowards."

"That was clear enough last night," said Vergil. "But are you not then one of these cowards as well?"

Bander blushed. "I am not proud of it, but I am in fact an operative for the city council working undercover with the KLAMP."

"A spy," said Vergil distastefully.

"As I said, I'm not proud of it, but in my defense I took the job only because I believed that the KLAMP represented a real threat to the stability of the city. After last night, however, I've concluded they are mostly harmless."

"Mostly?" asked Handri. "Then you do believe they pose some danger?"

"Yes," said Bander. "But not to the city."

"Then to whom?" asked Vergil.

"To *you*," said Bander. "Right now, the city council is preparing to call an emergency hearing about the KLAMP. They're determined to find some reason to disband the KLAMP and imprison its leaders."

"But nothing happened," Vergil protested.

"I know that," said Bander. "But the council is out for blood. They aren't going to be happy until someone is punished."

"Hold on," said Handri. "Are you saying they're going to go after *us*?"

"The council just wants to throw somebody in a dungeon," said Bander. "They don't care who. But you didn't make any friends in the KLAMP last night, and they've had all night to get their stories straight. I left shortly after you did, but they were already talking about making you two the scapegoats if the authorities went after them."

"Those cowardly bastards!" Vergil cried. "I'll not have my good name sullied in such a fashion!"

"The condition of your name will be the least of your worries if Collamer and his thugs get their way," said Bander. "Fortunately, there is still time to tell your side of the story. The council is summoning witnesses now. I was sent to fetch Collamer, in fact, but decided I had to warn you first. If you head over to the council chamber now, you can explain what happened before Collamer and the others have a chance to slander you. I can't keep the others from testifying, but you will have an advantage if you tell your side first."

"Why are you doing this?" asked Vergil. "Warning us, I mean?"

"To be honest," said Bander, "you've always been something of a hero to me. Although I bear no animosity toward goblins, the simple bravery of knights like you was an inspiration to me, and you were the last of your kind. I was disappointed when my first chance to meet you was at a gathering of a feckless vigilante group. But when you stood up to Collamer and the others, my faith was restored. I guess I figured I owed you this much, at least."

"It is much appreciated," said Vergil. "Is there anything we can do for you?"

"You need not do anything in return," said Bander. "Although I would make a couple of suggestions, for your own sake, if I'm not being presumptuous."

"Speak," said Vergil.

"Well," said Bander, "I realize that you were born in a different time, but I would strongly advise against making any prejudicial statements about goblins or other monsters. If the council thinks you harbor anti-goblin sentiment, they will be less likely to trust your word."

"Hmph," Vergil grunted. "And what else?"

"Go on the offensive against KLAMP," said Bander. "I realize that you are schooled in the ways of chivalry, and your natural inclination is to be as generous as possible to your enemies. But these are different times, and your enemies will grant you no such consideration. They will try to convince the council that the entire expedition was your idea, and that they stopped you from slaughtering the goblins. You must impress upon the council what a vile group of people these supposed knights really are if you are going to spare your name—not to mention your necks."

"I see," said Vergil.

"Well, I should get going. If I don't show up with Collamer soon, the council is going to suspect I'm up to something."

"Go then," said Vergil. "I thank you for your warning."

Bander bowed and left the room.

"What are we going to do?" asked Handri.

"There is only one thing *to* do," said Vergil. "I must go to this council and clear my name. You know the way, I take it?"

"Of course," said Handri. "But what do we even know about this Bander? How do we know he—"

"No time for dithering," snapped Vergil. "Get dressed and we'll be on our way."

Handri sighed but did not protest further. Half an hour later, they were walking through the city square toward the city council chambers.

"By Grovlik, what is that?" Vergil gasped, looking up at a massive figure towering over the center of the square.

"Oh, that's *Unity*," said Handri.

"*Unity?*" asked Vergil dubiously. The thing was vaguely humanoid-shaped, but featureless. It seemed to be made from granite, and was a good four stories tall.

"That's what they're calling it," said Handri. "It's supposed to represent all the races of Dis working together in harmony."

"It looks like a faceless abomination," said Vergil, with a shudder.

"I guess there were, um, creative differences," said Handri. "I think it was supposed to look like a combination of all the main races of Dis: humans, goblins, ogres and trolls. They dragged that big block of marble into the city so the sculptor's crew could work on it. They chipped away at the marble for twenty years, but just when it really started to take shape, everybody started bickering about it. The humans said that it should look more like a human than the other races, because there are more humans in Avaressa than monsters. And some humans thought it already looked monstrous because of how big it is, so the sculptor should make it look more human to compensate. A lot of goblins thought that it should look more like a goblin, though, because goblins have been the most discriminated against in Avaressa's history. The ogres threatened to stop chiseling if they couldn't make it look more like an ogre. Nobody really wanted it to look anything look a troll, but then they never would have gotten the block down from the mountains in the first place if it hadn't been for the trolls. Anyway, the ogres all quit a few years ago, and nobody on the council dares address the issue out of fear of offending one of the races. So it just looks like...*that*."

"It's *terrible*," Vergil said. "It would be better if they just picked any one of the races. Human, goblin, ogre, troll... Anything would be better than this." He paused, frowning at the bizarre figure in disgust. "Well, maybe not troll."

"But then it wouldn't symbolize unity," said Handri. "It has to look a little bit like everybody."

"Why?" asked Vergil. "All you're going to do is round off the edges of the features that make each race unique. Just pick one, for Grovlik's sake. This mixing of the races is unnatural!"

Several pedestrians—three humans and two goblins, to be precise—had stopped nearby and were now staring at Vergil with disapproval.

"We should probably get going," said Handri, glancing at them nervously. "Bander told us to go straight to the council."

"Very well," said Vergil. "I would just as soon get away from that ghastly amorphous visage in any case."

They made their way past the half-finished statue to the council building. They were stopped in the lobby by a bailiff, and Vergil demanded that he be allowed into the chamber.

"I'm sorry," said the bailiff. "Who are you again?"

"My name is Sir Vergil Parmeligo, Knight of the Order of the Unyielding Badger. Perhaps you have heard of me? I understand I am rather famous."

The bailiff shrugged apologetically. "The name doesn't ring any bells. What are you famous for exactly?"

"My faithful squire Salivar and I pursued a band of—" He stopped, recalling Bander's warning.

"You must have heard of him," Handri said. "He's the knight who slept for a hundred years."

"Ah!" cried the bailiff. "Of course. And did you by any chance have a stuffed weasel on your head while you slept?"

"A stuffed weasel?" asked Vergil, frowning. "Certainly not."

"That is unfortunate," the bailiff deadpanned, "as the bylaws clearly indicate that one is not owed an audience with the city council merely for sleeping a hundred years unless one has had, during his slumber, a stuffed weasel on his head."

"What an absurd rule," said Vergil.

"So it would seem," replied the bailiff. "If it were up to me, I'd admit anyone who had slept for at least a fortnight, but I don't make the rules."

"See here," said Vergil, beginning to lose his temper. "I demand the opportunity to clear my name before this council!"

"Clear your name?" asked the bailiff. "Sir, I'm intimately familiar with the business of the council, and I can assure you that your name has never once come up. The only thing clearer than your name as far as this body is concerned is the ether."

"That is only because my enemies have not yet had a chance to slander me," said Vergil.

"So you are requesting the opportunity to preemptively clear your name against future slanders?" asked the bailiff.

"Precisely!" declared Vergil. "I have it on good authority that this body will soon be interviewing witnesses regarding certain recent events centering on a group of goblin refugees, and I have reason to believe that several of those witnesses are conspiring to spread lies against me."

"Well," said the bailiff, "when and if those lies are told, I'll be certain to—"

But he broke off as a tall, thin man in a fine suit exited the chamber behind him. "What's going on out here, Yedrik? Someone told me that…" The man's eyes went to Vergil. "Good heavens!" he cried. "You must be Sir Vergil!"

"I am indeed," said Vergil, with a contemptuous glare at the bailiff, who reddened visibly.

"I am Thameril, the mayor of Avaressa. I had heard you woke up, but I wasn't sure whether to believe it. It is an honor to meet you, sir. You are quite well-known and respected in these parts— and throughout Dis, I would imagine."

Vergil accepted these accolades with aplomb as the bailiff turned an even brighter shade of red, but he couldn't help wondering where such admirers were when he was asleep in a dilapidated house with a servant who had to resort to severing his limbs in an attempt to buy food.

"On any ordinary day I would of course be more than happy to meet with you and catch you up on the latest goings-on in town," Thameril went on, "but as it happens, the council is about to start an emergency session on a pressing problem that has come up." Vergil couldn't help notice that Thameril seemed anxious, and dark circles under his eyes indicated that he had not slept well of late.

"Actually," said Vergil, "that is precisely why I am here. My servant and I happened to be present during certain events that unfolded last night, and I believe I can offer some insight into what occurred."

"You two were with the Knights for the Limitation of the Advancement of Monstrous Populations last night?" asked Thameril.

"Handri's allegiance is to me," said Vergil, "and as my order has dissolved, mine is only to my own sense of honor. It is true, however, that we were physically present during last night's events, as the result of the efforts of that rogue Collamer's attempts to enlist us. We remain unaffiliated with the vigilantes, though, and in fact it was only our presence among them that prevented matters from escalating to wholesale slaughter."

Thameril nodded, taking this all in. "Yedrik," he said to the bailiff, "could you give us a moment?"

The bailiff shrugged and left the antechamber.

"I know of this Collamer," Thameril said. "You're saying he's the leader of the KLAMP?"

"That is my understanding," said Vergil.

"And he never spoke to you of anyone else pulling the strings of the KLAMP? Someone, say, in a position of power in the local government who channels funds to them and provides them with sensitive information?"

"He spoke of no such person," said Vergil. "Are you saying that you suspect the KLAMP has a high-placed contact in the city government?"

"Rumors to that effect have been circulating lately," said Thameril, looking about nervously although there was no one else in the room. "Of course, if such a person existed, he would probably keep his identity hidden from the others in the KLAMP.

And knowing Collamer, if he knew the identity of this person, he would have bragged to you about him."

"If there is anyone pulling Collamer's strings," said Vergil, "I'm afraid I remain ignorant of the matter."

"Very good," said Thameril, looking somewhat relieved. "I mean, it's very good that you've come to me with what you know. Certain members of the council seem to have it in for the KLAMP, and while I'm a strong defender of the right of free association of our citizens, I'm afraid we can't have bands of armed vigilantes intimidating innocent goblins. Don't you agree?"

Vergil had to bite his tongue to avoid objecting to the phrase "innocent goblins," which struck him as an oxymoron. "My main concern," he said, dodging Thameril's question, "is to preserve my good name against any charges these men may make against me."

Thameril smiled. "Oh, I quite understand," he said. "I believe our interests are aligned, Sir Vergil. We would like to see the law deal justly and swiftly with the KLAMP while avoiding the temptation to sully the names of others who are, at most, only tangentially involved in their activities. Would you say that is accurate?"

"I suppose so," replied Vergil.

"Good!" exclaimed Thameril. "Then let's get you in front of the council."

Thameril escorted Vergil into the chamber, insisting that Handri remain outside. Handri tried to object, but Vergil assured him that he could speak for both of them. Thameril introduced Vergil to the other eight members of the council—three of which, Vergil saw to his dismay, were goblins. One of these held a long, ornately carved staff with a small silver globe at its head. The names of the other council members didn't persist in Vergil's memory more than a few seconds, but the name of the goblin with the staff stuck: he was called Grimble.

The council members all seemed to be at least vaguely familiar with Vergil's story, although a few were surprised to learn that he was an actual person, and not merely a figure in some half-forgotten legend. The council members were generally deferential, with the exception of Grimble, who seemed suspicious of him. Thameril asked Vergil a series of leading questions, prompting him to give his account of what had transpired the previous night. Despite Bander's urging to go on the offensive, Vergil's tendency was toward self-deprecation and a refusal to disparage Collamer and his gang. But Thameril cut him off when he would try to qualify his own admirable actions and drew him out whenever he said anything remotely critical of the Knights for the Limitation of the Advancement of Monstrous Populations, so that although it was not his intention, Vergil's testimony painted a picture of Vergil as a reluctant hero rescuing a group of harried refugees from a band of bloodthirsty thugs. On one hand, Vergil was pleased at how well his testimony was going, but on the other, he didn't like feeling that he was a pawn of a political agenda he didn't understand.

When Thameril at last opened up the floor for cross-examination, Grimble pounced. "Correct me if I misheard you," he said, "but you claimed to be that very same Vergil who fell into a coma one hundred and three years ago as the result of an accident involving zelaznium, did you not?"

"I am he," said Vergil.

"And how is it that you are still alive?" asked the goblin.

"That is not for me to say," said Vergil. "It has been conjectured that in addition to suppressing wakefulness, the zelaznium I inhaled also inhibited my natural aging process. Thus while I have experienced only forty years of life, and have the appearance of a man in his seventies, I am in fact, one hundred forty three years old."

"And yet you expect us to believe that even at the ripe old age of 143, you are in full command of your wits?"

"I have no expectations on the matter one way or another," said Vergil. "I myself am surprised enough to find that I remain, for the most part, in command of my bladder."

Chuckles arose from the group, and Grimble scowled. "For those of us who haven't heard the legend," he went on, "how was it that you fell into this supposed coma?"

"I know nothing of legends," said Vergil, "but I can tell you what precipitated my lengthy slumber. I was chasing a band of go... that is, of bandits who had broken into the laboratory of the alchemist Zelaznus and stolen a pouch of the silvery powder that is now called zelaznium. While attempting to recover said zelaznium, I accidentally inhaled a great deal of it. I woke up a hundred years later."

"I see," said Grimble. "And what was the racial makeup of these bandits?"

Thameril stood up to object. "I don't see what that has to do with anything," he said. "Besides, the facts of the case are well-documented. Sir Vergil is hardly to blame for the fact that the thieves in this case were goblins."

"I merely wish to determine whether the witness' testimony is slanted by anti-goblin bias."

"Then ask your question directly," said Thameril. "No need to bring up ancient history. Although if you do intend to dwell on the distant past, let me remind you that the band of goblins Vergil pursued is widely believed to have been a band of mercenaries employed by a *human* magician. So perhaps you should consider the possibility that Vergil harbors anti-human bias as well."

Vergil raised an eyebrow at this. As far as he knew, the goblins had been working alone. But of course it made sense that someone had hired them to steal the zelaznium.

"Ah yes," said Grimble with a smirk. "The legendary illusionist Quandrasi, who was so skilled at his trade that no one has ever actually seen him. Isn't it strange how goblins are blamed for every sort of evil, but are apparently so dimwitted that even their most diabolical plans still require human supervision?"

"You're out of order, Grimble," said Thameril. "We appreciate your efforts to combat anti-goblin discrimination, but I will thank you to remain on topic."

"Fine," said Grimble. "Vergil, do you hate goblins?"

Vergil was momentarily speechless. Of *course* he hated goblins. Every sane person of his generation hated goblins. But how could he explain that to this group? He doubted he could even make the humans understand, to say nothing of the goblins present. These people, who had grown up with goblins doing their dishes and weeding their gardens, could never understand the threat the subhumanoid races had once posed—the threat that he believed they still posed, if he were honest. But if the threat remained, then it behooved him to keep his sentiments secret. And of course his credibility with the council would dissolve completely if he admitted to hating goblins. They would take the word of Collamer and the other "knights" over his, he would be sent to the dungeon, and his name would be sullied forever.

While he was deliberating on his answer, the door to the chamber opened and the bailiff escorted in five men: Collamer and four of the other members of the KLAMP. They glared at Vergil, who did his best to ignore them.

"Of course I don't hate goblins," said Vergil. "I pursued those bandits only because they absconded with a priceless supply of zelaznium and abducted Zelaznus himself. My actions were in no way motivated by the race of the thieves." The lie settled in his gut like a pound of sand, but what choice did he have?

"And how was it that you happened to be with this anti-goblin group last night?"

"I was invited along, not knowing the character of the men or the purpose of the group," said Vergil, glancing at Collamer, who stared back at him. "As I already stated, as soon as I realized the group intended to harm the goblin refugees, I opposed them so that the goblins could move freely."

"You're quite the hero, then, aren't you?" Grimble asked.

Vergil shrugged. "I did what I thought was right." That much, at least, was true.

"Who is the leader of this organization?" Grimble asked.

"As far as I know, a man named Collamer."

"As far as you know?"

Vergil glanced momentarily at Thameril, who seemed to be very interested in something on the ceiling. "I know little of the organizational structure of the group," he said. "Collamer is the man who approached me, and for all intents and purposes he appeared to be their leader. Collamer claimed to be merely an organizer, and he expressed a desire to recruit me to lead them. I passed on the honor."

"And do you see this Collamer here in this chamber?"

"I do," said Vergil. "That is he, standing near the door." He pointed at Collamer.

"And do you recognize the other men with him?"

"They are other members of the Knights for the Limitation of the Advancement of Monstrous Populations," said Vergil.

"They are, in fact, the leaders of that organization, are they not?"

Vergil shrugged. "If you say so."

Grimble looked for a moment as if he was going to ask something else, but then thought better of it. "I think we've heard enough," he said.

Thameril stood up, looking relieved. "Thank you very much, Sir Vergil," he said. "That is all this council requires of you at present."

Vergil nodded and got to his feet. He felt nearly as tired and worn out as he had the day he awoke from his hundred-year slumber. Lying did not suit a Knight of the Order of the Unyielding Badger. His only consolation was that the key elements of his testimony were true. He could not prevent the other witnesses from slandering him, but at least he had spoken his side of the story. He wondered if he should have done more to discredit Collamer and the others, but there was nothing to be done about it now. He didn't like having his testimony go up against that of five conspirators—and commoners, at that!—but he was beginning to accept that there were many things about this new world that he could not control. He would just hope that the council would be able to weigh the evidence fairly and discern the truth.

As he made his way to the door, Thameril was leaning over Grimble, and the two seemed to be locked in intense discussion. Eventually they came to some kind of agreement. Grimble leaned back in his chair, a smile playing on his face, as Thameril stood up again to address the council. Presumably he would call Collamer and the other men as witnesses, and Vergil considered staying to hear them out, but there was no point: he'd said his part; the rest was up to the council. He had his hand on the doorknob as Thameril spoke:

"Bailiff, please place these five men under arrest."

Ten

"What happened?" Handri asked. "What is going on?"

Vergil flopped onto the couch, tired and bewildered. Handri had been pestering him for answers since he had walked out of the council chamber, but Vergil had been too stunned to answer.

"Sir, please talk to me," Handri pleaded. "What happened with the council? Are we in trouble?"

Vergil shook his head. "No, Handri," he managed to murmur. "We are safe. For now, anyway."

"Then what happened?"

"To be entirely honest," said Vergil, "I don't know *what* happened. The more I think about it, the less certain I am about anything that has happened since I woke up nearly a month ago."

"Well, you can be certain of one thing," said Handri. "I'm your friend. And your servant."

Vergil frowned. "That's two things."

"It feels like one," said Handri. "I can't separate the two in my head."

"Fair enough, good Handri," said Vergil. "You are right, you have given me no reason to doubt you. Allow me to give you my account of the meeting, and perhaps together we can make sense of it." He proceeded to tell Handri about his interrogation by Thameril and Grimble.

"Hmm," said Handri. "Sounds to me like you got off easy. That is, *we* got off easy."

"Quite," said Vergil. "That council was ready to string up anybody who had an ounce of anti-goblin sentiment in his body, but somehow I was allowed to walk free. Meanwhile, the rest of the KLAMP leadership is presumably languishing in a dungeon somewhere. I cannot help thinking that I was playing a part in a drama that had been scripted for me."

"Scripted by whom?" asked Handri.

"Would that I knew, Handri!" cried Vergil. "Before I fell into my unfortunate slumber I considered myself possessed of an incisive wit and a solid grasp of chivalric principles, but I seem to be able to rely on neither anymore. I feel like a newborn foal, blinking and quivering in the sunlight, being led blindly from one cause to another. And while I am not particularly aggrieved regarding the fate of those cotton-heads of the KLAMP, I resent being used in this way. Somehow I've gone from being a champion against the goblins to being a weapon in the goblin arsenal against humans."

"I wonder," said Handri, rubbing his chin thoughtfully. "Is it truly the goblins that are plotting against you, or is it merely this Grimble character? I know you are convinced of the wickedness of goblins and ogres, but in my experience no ordinary monster can match the level of depravity that seems to be the minimal qualification to become a politician."

"Well, it couldn't just have been Grimble," said Vergil. "I am not familiar with the rules of such a council, but they seem to have come to a consensus that the KLAMP were to be prosecuted."

"That's what I'm saying," replied Handri. "You said there were only three goblins on the council out of nine. So it's not just the goblins who had a grudge against the KLAMP."

"True," said Vergil thoughtfully. "Now that you mention it, while there was clearly no love lost between Grimble and the mayor, Thameril, toward the end it seemed almost as though they had a compromise between them. And there was something else strange about Thameril. He seemed very eager to get the whole business over with."

"You think the mayor has been secretly working with the KLAMP?"

Vergil frowned. His mind actually hadn't made that leap yet, but he wasn't going to admit it to Handri. "That would explain why he didn't want them to testify. He sacrificed his pawns rather than risk the truth coming out."

"As you say, though," Handri noted, "it is hardly a tragedy that the leaders of the KLAMP have been thrown in a dungeon. Given their violent tendencies and willingness to take the law into their own hands, I suspect that it would have happened eventually, with or without your testimony. And who knows what mayhem they may have caused if they were allowed to continue."

"Perhaps," said Vergil. "And yet, part of me suspects that the KLAMP was all talk, as we used to say. For all their bluster, the closest they came to actually attacking a goblin was Collamer's poorly executed charge, which you had little difficulty countering. I suspect he never intended to do more than scare them. They were relying on me to make the first move against the goblins, and when I balked, they put up virtually no resistance."

"Still," said Handri, "if you're going to ride around on horseback with swords, trying to scare the wits out of innocent goblins, you can hardly complain when you get thrown in a dungeon."

There was that phrase again. *Innocent goblins.* Vergil wondered if there really was such a thing. "In any case," Handri went on, "the matter is settled now."

"I hope so," Vergil said, but doubts gnawed at him. He saw the malevolent look on Grimble's face during his interrogation. That goblin had more on his mind than jailing a few troublemakers.

"At least those vigilantes have a place to sleep," said Handri. "Now that we're once again unemployed, we have no such guarantee."

Vergil groaned. Why had he awoken into this strange new world where there clearly was no place for him? His customs were outdated, his principles useless, his skills worthless, his honor meaningless. Every time he set out to right some wrong, he somehow managed to make things worse.

"So what do we do now?" asked Handri.

"There is only one thing *to* do," said Vergil, standing up decisively. "We are going to get drunk."

They went downstairs and made their way to a nearby tavern, where the spent the next several hours doing just that. Handri halfheartedly objected to spending a good chunk of their remaining money on wine, but Vergil overruled him, arguing that all sobriety had gotten them over the past few days was trouble. They commiserated at gradually escalating volume, and Vergil had a vague recollection of being tossed out of the tavern after an attempt at leading the patrons in a chorus of "Hollick the Goblin-Slayer," an enchanting ballad whose lyrics went:

> Hollick, do you hear it?
> That distant goblin chant
> Put away your spirits
> Get up and don your pants
>
> Hollick, don't be tardy
> The brutes are at the gate
> You are brave and you are hardy
> For once please don't be late
>
> Hollick, good to see you
> Our men are mostly dead
> Was it the screams of the wounded
> That got you out of bed?
>
> Hollick, we're victorious!
> You've really saved the day
> How fortunate you're with us
> Or it would've happened anyway
>
> Hollick, I am wounded
> My blood's spilling on the floor
> So I give to you this ballad
> I haven't got much more
>
> Hollick, my song is finished
> You know that it is true
> I have but one regret, and that
> Is naming it for you

Vergil knew several even more virulently anti-goblin songs, but this one was enough to get him and Handri thrown into the street. That was probably just as well, because by that time they'd already imbibed near-toxic quantities of alcohol. At some point, they must have made their way back to the apartment, because sometime late the next day (judging by the angle of the sunlight through the windows) Vergil awoke to banging on the front door. Again.

He groaned and got to his feet, holding his head in his hands. The banging persisted. He stumbled across the bedroom past Handri, still asleep on the couch, and opened the door. Ordinarily, he'd have made some effort to determine who was on the other side first, but he couldn't bring himself to raise his voice to the level required to be heard through the door. If someone was here to kill him, he just hoped that they got it over with quickly. As the door opened, he shuffled to the couch, shoved Handri's legs out of the way, and slumped down next to him.

"Ahh?" Handri murmured, sitting up in time to see a burly, well-dressed man stroll into the apartment: Marko, Lord Balphry himself.

Vergil groaned. "What do *you* want? I have nothing left to steal."

Marko regarded him piteously. "What I want," he said, "is to know what in Dis is going on in this town."

"Eh?" asked Vergil.

Marko sighed and walked to the window. He opened it, and the room was flooded with the sounds of commotion: panicked horses whinnying, angry shouts, a woman's scream, some kind of alarm clanging in the distance. "The whole city has gone crazy," said Marko, shaking his head. "There's no escaping the cage."

Vergil and Handri exchanged puzzled glances. "I'm sorry," said Vergil. "To what cage are you referring?"

"CAGE," said Marko. "The Committee for Advancing Goblin Equality. They're swearing in a bunch of unemployed goblins as deputies and sending them out in the city to arrest anyone they think is sympathetic to the Knights for the Limitation of the Advancement of Monstrous Populations. Grimble is at the head of it, and he's out for blood."

"You're saying," Handri mused, "that the CAGE captain is clamping down on the KLAMP camp?"

"That is exactly what I'm saying," said Marko, unamused by Handri's alliteration. "What in Grovlik's name have you done, Vergil?"

"I resent the implication that this 'CAGE' organization is somehow my fault." Vergil said. "Further, you have quite a bit of nerve to come into my apartment and make accusations after bilking me out of everything I own."

"This is *my apartment*, you idiot," Marko snapped. "I could toss you both out on your ears right now if I felt like it. Now talk. What did you do?"

Vergil thrust out his chin defiantly. "I haven't the faintest idea what you're talking about."

"Then you didn't testify before the city council yesterday?"

"I merely offered my account of certain events the previous night, in order to ensure the preservation of my good name."

"Your account? Don't tell me you were with those morons in the KLAMP the other night."

"Only on a provisional basis," Vergil said. "They were attempting to head off a band of goblin refugees who were en route to the city. Handri and I successfully defused the situation."

Marko rubbed his scalp with his palm and groaned. "You didn't *defuse* anything. You *escalated* the situation. Until yesterday, everybody thought the KLAMP was a big joke. A few idiots who liked to ride around on horses and act tough. Now people are talking about them like there are KLAMP agents hiding behind every corner. CAGE is serious. They're arresting people on the flimsiest of evidence. If you've ever told a joke about goblins and somebody rats you out, you'll be lucky to avoid being thrown in the dungeon."

"That's absurd," said Vergil, wondering what those running CAGE would have made of his rendition of "Hollick the Goblin Slayer" the previous night.

"You can't really think *we're* to blame for all that," said Handri, frowning.

Marko sighed. "What you two morons don't understand," he said, "is that monster-human relations are a very delicate matter in this city. Generally, everybody gets along with everybody, but there are fringe elements on both sides just itching to cause trouble. Your stunt at the mill sent a wave of goblin refugees into town, when it's already absorbing about as many new workers as it possibly can. That got the KLAMP all worked up. Usually they don't do more than talk, and KLAMP's leadership seems to have some political connections that helped them avoid serious legal consequences so far. But apparently you managed to provoke them into causing enough trouble that the council couldn't ignore them anymore. And the council probably figured they couldn't very well ignore the testimony of a living legend such as yourself, so they threw the leaders in the dungeon and formed the CAGE to root out the remaining members. That no-good schemer Grimble had the charter for the CAGE already written, and the council rubber-stamped it without taking time to read the fine print. Turns out the CAGE is empowered to enlist an unlimited number of volunteers to help it locate 'anti-goblin extremists,' a term which it left deliberately up to interpretation. These "volunteers" get a bounty for each extremist they turn in, and—again, thanks to you—there is a ready pool of unemployed goblins for the CAGE to recruit. The volunteers have almost no training or education, and they don't have a clue how to identify the KLAMP members, so they've been wreaking havoc in the city."

"Why doesn't the council put a stop to it?" asked Vergil. "Where is the city guard?"

"The city guard has been ordered to cooperate with the CAGE. The council is so worried about goblin unrest that they are reluctant to appear as if they are giving in to anti-goblin extremists. Now that they've identified the KLAMP as an extremist organization, they're committed to rooting them out. But these goblins are causing so much trouble, I wouldn't be surprised if they're actually prompting *more* people to join the KLAMP. The whole thing is such a disaster, it's almost as if somebody planned the whole thing to create as much mayhem as possible. But apparently there's no mastermind behind it. Every idiotic step in the process leads back to you."

"Why do you even care about this CAGE/KLAMP claptrap?" Handri asked. "Why don't you just stay at your estate and wait it out?"

Marko glared at him. "I care," he said, "because it affects my investments. Factories are shutting down. Shipments are being delayed. Orders are not being placed. If this keeps up, I'll be ruined!"

"You seem to think that this fact is of interest to us," said Vergil.

"Look," said Marko. "I understand your animosity toward me. That was a tough break with the mill. But you *did* burn it down. It's hardly fair that I should bear the loss."

"I have accepted my losses," Vergil said. "Just as you no doubt will accept yours. There is nothing I can do about the political situation in the city now, even if I were so inclined."

"You can go back to the council, try to talk some sense into them," said Marko. "Use your celebrity to put an end to this madness before matters get completely out of hand."

"If what you say about the current state of affairs is true," said Vergil, "it would seem futile to attempt to stuff the cat back in the bag, so to speak. Perhaps if I had not been so poorly advised regarding the political situation in the first place, I might have made better use of my opportunity to speak to the council. I am afraid, however, that that time has passed."

"Vergil, I will admit that I'm partly to blame for the way things have gone," said Marko. "But I'm asking you to put your grudge against me aside for a moment, if not for my sake or the sake of the city, then in the interest of preserving your good name. You don't want to be remembered as the man who precipitated the decline of Avaress into riots and anarchy."

"It seems to me," said Vergil, "that every time I intervene— either out of chivalric principles or concern for my good name—I succeed in making things worse. I am coming to the conclusion that neither my name nor my principles are worth much in this strange new world in which I find myself. There is no longer any honor among the aristocracy, as you have clearly demonstrated, and what passes for a "knight" these days is a slovenly shopkeeper brandishing a potato peeler. Cities and countries are ruled not by noblemen but by petty bureaucrats who are as greedy as they are short-sighted. Why, not even the depravity of goblins can be relied upon anymore. The noble has been debased and the monstrous has become commonplace. No, Marko, I shall expend no more effort in defense either of my name or of my vaunted principles. For the foreseeable future, I plan to stay out of the affairs of both men and goblins, except insofar as self-preservation requires."

"Then speak up in your own self-interest!" cried Marko. "If the state of affairs continues to deteriorate, you will not remain untouched by the violence in this city. And speaking more immediately, don't forget that you stay in this apartment only as long as I allow it. I had intended on letting you stay through the end of this week, but I could certainly extend your lease by a few months—or shorten it."

"So at last you are reduced to naked bribery," said Vergil. "I expected no less. What do you suggest? That I grovel in front of the council, pleading for them to disband the Committee, in return for being allowed to stay here for another month? No, Marko, even if I trusted you to uphold your end of the bargain, which I do not, I would not debase myself so. If I am reduced to selling my services, then I will do so honestly. Perhaps I will become a blacksmith or a street sweeper."

"Don't be stupid, Vergil. You're acting against your own self-interest just to spite me."

"I see we understand each other," Vergil replied.

Marko glared at him. "Indeed," he said. "What fools men of your day must have been. It's a wonder we survived your generation at all. Well, since you seem to have no intention of cleaning up your mess, I suppose I will have to stay in town and manage things myself." He walked to the door and opened it. "Yurgi!" he snapped. "Bring my bags upstairs."

"You're moving in *here*?" asked Handri.

"It's where I typically stay when I have business in town," said Marko. "The fact that you two get thrown onto the street is an added bonus. And although I doubt I would have any trouble evicting a decrepit old knight and his monkey-faced gardener, Yurgi should be able to convince you that resisting is not in your best interests. She can be quite persuasive."

They heard heavy footsteps coming up the stairs.

"She?" asked Handri.

"Yurgi is my bouncer and general purpose enforcer," said Marko. "I usually don't travel with servants, but I find that having Yurgi around often helps to eliminate a certain amount of ambiguity in business transactions. For example, you may be wondering what exactly I meant when I said I would have you thrown onto the street. Perhaps, you think, Lord Balphry has lapsed into speaking in idioms. Yurgi will be only too happy to clarify the matter for you. Won't you, Yurgi?"

As he spoke, a hulking figure appeared in the doorway. Or, more precisely, the lower two-thirds of it appeared. It was roughly human-shaped, but it had to be at least nine feet tall, with limbs like tree trunks. As it bent over to peer into the apartment, beady eyes staring stupidly out from beneath a massive brow, Vergil realized with a shudder that the creature was indeed female. Great, pendulous breasts hung nearly to its waist, nipples mercifully covered by a bedsheet that had been fashioned into a makeshift toga. Its dirty blond hair was pulled into twin ponytails on the side of its head. In each hand the ogre gripped the handles of three suitcases. A putrid smell like curdled milk and composting onions preceded her into the room. "Huh?" the ogre said.

"I was just explaining to these gentlemen how helpful you are, dear," said Marko.

"Oh," said Yurgi. "Yeah, sure, boss. That's me. Where do you want these?"

"Just drop them anywhere," said Marko.

Yurgi dropped the suitcases.

"Inside the apartment, you nitwit," said Marko.

"Oh, right." Yurgi picked up the suitcases and brought them inside, bending almost in half to get through the opening. Her shoulders barely fit through the doorway. She set the suitcases on the floor. "Who are these guys, boss?" she said, examining Vergil and Handri.

"Previous tenants," said Marko. "I'm going to get some dinner. See that these two are cleared out by the time I get back, won't you, Yurgi?"

"Sure, boss," said Yurgi. "You gonna bring me back something?"

"You can get something to eat after I get back."

"Screech melons?" asked the ogre hopefully.

"No!" cried Marko. "What did I tell you about that?"

"Screech melons rot my teeth."

"That's watermelons."

"Screech melons make my face itch."

"That's walnuts."

"Screech melons make my bottom—"

"Yurgi!" Marko snapped. "Screech melons don't *do* anything."

"'Cept be delicious," said Yurgi, a rapturous smile creeping across her face.

"What I mean," said Marko irritably, "is that the reason you can't eat screech melons has nothing to do with what they *do*."

"Then why *can't* I?"

"I've explained this before, Yurgi. I'm not doing it again. No screech melons."

Yurgi pouted silently.

"What are screech melons?" asked Handri.

"You don't want to know," said Marko. "I wish I didn't. Good day, Vergil." Marko spun on his heel and walked to the door.[3]

"So, um, I guess you guys need to leave," said Yurgi. After a pause, she smacked her fist into her palm, as if remembering that she was supposed to be making an effort to appear intimidating. Vergil got the impression that Yurgi didn't particularly enjoy being hired muscle, but there probably weren't a lot of other career options open to her. Vergil had never seen an ogre up close before, and it was oddly disconcerting to meet one—particularly a female— under these circumstances. As vile and fearsome as ogres were in the wild, seeing one dressed in a toga and doing the bidding of a petty aristocrat like Marko seemed rather pathetic. Vergil was under no illusions about the ogre's physical capabilities, however, and wasn't eager to find out how Yurgi would interpret Marko's instruction to "toss them into the street." He and Handri gathered their things and made their way to the door.

"You need any help down?" asked Yurgi.

---

[3] You probably don't want to know either, but in case you do, you can find the answer in *Disenchanted*. These footnotes seem to be developing a theme.

"I think we can manage!" yelped Vergil, with a little more enthusiasm than was necessary.

Yurgi shrugged. "It was nice to meet you," she said, with what seemed to be a sincere—although horrifying—smile.

Vergil and Handri did their best to smile back and ran down the stairs.

"Seems like a nice girl," said Handri, as they exited onto the street.

"That ogre would tear you apart as soon as look at you," said Vergil.

"Sure," said Handri with a shrug. "But that's true of all ogres. You can't hold it against Yurgi."

"She works for that lying bastard Marko," said Vergil. "That's enough reason to hold it against her."

"I suppose," said Handri, as the two began walking down the street. After some time, Handri spoke again. "I appreciate your anger toward Lord Balphry," he said, "and I fully support your decision not to be in his debt, but I can't help observing that we are almost out of money and have no place to sleep tonight. Sir, what are we going to do?"

Vergil sighed. "I have absolutely no idea."

Eleven

"I need a drink," said Vergil as he and Handri made their way down the street. "Seeing an ogre draped in a bedsheet is unnatural. And that *smell*."

"A drink would certainly help us get over the odor of the toga'd ogre," said Handri, "but we have maybe enough money left for two solid meals, and you're still hungover from last night."

"That's two more reasons to drink," said Vergil.

"No more drinking," said Handri. "I'm sorry, sir, I must insist. We need to be clear-headed if we're ever going to figure a way out of this mess."

As he spoke, a terrified-looking young man ran past them and ducked into an alley. A moment later two goblins ran down the street, stopping in front of them. "You seen a guy run down this way?" one of them asked.

"N—" Handri started.

"Indeed we have," Vergil interjected. "He ran right past us and into that building on the left. I'd check the apartment on the top floor if I were you."

"Much appreciated, citizen!" said the goblin, and the two ran toward Marko's apartment. Vergil and Handri watched as the goblins threw open the door and disappeared up the stairs.

"Why did you do that?" asked Handri. "Are you trying to make enemies of this goblin committee, whatever it's called?"

"CAGE," said Vergil. "I suppose my curiosity got the better of me."

"Curiosity?" asked Handri. "About what?"

"Well, I wanted to see if...."

They watched as two goblins flew out the window of the apartment and landed with a crunch on a pile of refuse below. The goblins lay moaning in pain.

"That wasn't very sporting," said Handri.

"No, I suppose not," said Vergil. "But rooting out dissidents is dangerous work. It will toughen them up for their next adventure." Yurgi appeared at the window and looked down at the two goblins, who were grumbling and staggering to their feet. The ogre caught sight of Vergil and Handri and waved. They waved back.

"All right, no wine," said Vergil. "But let's get something to eat."

"Again, allow me to point out that we've got enough money for maybe two more meals," said Handri.

"Then I propose we have one of them now," said Vergil.

Handri sighed but didn't argue. Unfortunately, the only place they could find to acquire food nearby was the tavern they'd been thrown out of the previous night. Handri was convinced returning there was a bad idea given the agitated state of affairs in the city, but it was getting dark and Vergil insisted it wasn't safe to walk the city streets at night—which was probably also true. In the end, Handri relented.

Fortunately, the place was crowded and dimly lit, so the proprietor didn't take a second look at them. They ordered beer and food, and he simply nodded and returned to the kitchen.

"Things will be all right, Handri," said Vergil. "You will see."

"Are you sure?" Handri asked. "You sounded rather pessimistic back at the apartment."

"That was a mere setback," said Vergil. "We've had a string of bad luck lately, but fortunately for you, I am a man of superior breeding and possessed of a comprehensive chivalric education. Altering our luck is merely a matter of adopting the appropriate mental attitude."

"So you have an idea for making some money?" Handri asked hopefully.

"Do not be so limited in your thinking, Handri. Has it occurred to you that your preoccupation with money is the reason you never have any of it? In any case, we will be in a better position to adopt the appropriate attitude once we have partaken of some food. What is keeping that man, anyway?"

As he was speaking, a buxom young wench who had been sitting nearby stumbled over, slamming into their table. "Sorry!" she exclaimed. "I just had to come over and say hello. Aren't you that knight? The famous one who was sleeping for so long?"

"Sir Vergil Parmeligo at your service, miss," said Vergil. "Does your father know where you are?"

"My *father?*" the girl said. "That's a weird thing to say." She turned to Handri. "Your famous sleeping friend is *weird.*"

"So I've noticed," said Handri.

"My dear," said Vergil, "if you require an escort home, I would be more than happy to—"

"Hey everybody," the girl shouted suddenly. "It's that sleeping knight!" Then she burst into laughter. "Get it? Sleeping. Knight. Oh my goodness, your shameless freaking friend is slow funny!"

Several people at nearby tables, taking notice of the girl's performance, began glancing at Vergil and murmuring amongst themselves.

"Sir," Handri said nervously, "I think we ought to leave. We're drawing a great deal of attention. If what Lord Balphry said about CAGE is true…"

"Don't be silly, Handri," Vergil said. "We haven't even gotten our food yet."

The girl leaned heavily on the table, her blouse spilling open to allow Vergil to see straight down to her navel. "Don't *leave*, Sleeping Knight and Sleeping Knight's silly friend!"

A wiry man with short gray hair and a stern face got up from another table nearby. "You were in here last night," he said with a scowl. "Singing about killing goblins, you were." He glanced behind him at a table halfway across the room that was occupied by a party of six goblins. The goblins had been minding their own business, but their ears perked up at the old man's words.

"I think your memory fails you," said Vergil. "As a recent addition to the ranks of the elderly myself, I can empathize. Have a seat, good sir, and I will buy you a beer."

"He's right," said a woman at another table. "They was in here, singin' about how they was gonna kill goblins."

"Nonsense!" exclaimed Vergil. "That song recounts the goblin assault on Avaressa nearly two hundred years ago. It is highly inaccurate to characterize it as an ode to goblin-killing. If you want to hear a really anti-goblin song, you have to go back to the classic 'There's a Goblin in the Woodshed (Burn it Down, Burn it Down)' or perhaps 'The Finest Goblin I Know,' which describes an incident in which a goblin fell into a meat grinder."

The room went silent. Even the tipsy girl standing next to their table was staring at Vergil in horror.

"I am merely trying to put things in perspective," Vergil explained, glancing nervously at the table of goblins. "You people don't know what real prejudice is like." He paused for a moment, and somehow the room became even quieter than it had been. "And when I say 'you people,'" he went on, "I'm referring to those of you who get your knickers in a bunch over a silly song about goblin-killing. I don't mean 'you people,' as in goblins—who are not, strictly speaking, people."

Every eye in the place was now on Vergil. Handri was doing his best to appear invisible. Vergil realized he had gone too far to back down now.

"Look," he said, pushing his chair away and standing up. "I will be the first to acknowledge that some of my attitudes are old-fashioned, and that I have at times been less than charitable in my thinking toward the lesser races, but by the same token I possess a perspective that you good people lack. It is clear to me that many of your current problems have arisen precisely because of your misguided ideology regarding goblins and other sorts of monsters. This paranoia regarding anti-goblin sentiment that currently pervades the city—and, if I am not misreading the situation, seems to extend to the present company—obviously arises from the misguided belief that the various races can coexist peacefully in the same city. Now perhaps there is some place for subhumanoids on the fringes of society, working jobs that are menial, dangerous, undignified, or otherwise unsuitable for human beings, but it is readily apparent that monsters simply don't have the intelligence or skill for more important positions. There's no telling what sort of havoc might ensue if you start putting goblins in charge of things."

"Aren't you the guy who burned down the Goblintex mill?" asked someone in the vicinity of the goblins' table.

"That was an accident!" cried Vergil.

As he spoke, the door to the tavern opened and two rough-looking goblins hobbled in. They looked like they had just been rolling around in a pile of garbage.

"There they are!" cried one of them. "Seize those two!"

"Uh-oh," said Handri.

Vergil made a split-second calculation. On one hand, chivalry frowned on running from a battle. On the other hand, Vergil and Handri were badly outnumbered and unarmed, having been ordered to remove their swords at the door. Ultimately Vergil decided that perhaps in the current century certain exceptions to the code of chivalry had to be made.

"Run!" Vergil cried. He spun around and ran toward the rear of the room, hoping to find a back exit. Handri was close on his heels. Vergil ran with his arms out in front of him, prepared to shove his way through the crowd, but most of those in his way stepped back as he came through. For all their disapproval of Vergil's comments about monsters, there didn't seem to be a lot of enthusiasm for assisting CAGE. Vergil located a door and threw it open, finding himself in a dark alley. Handri nearly bowled him over as Vergil stopped a moment to assess their options. To their left the alley let out onto a street lit with gas lamps on posts; to their right the alley disappeared into darkness. It would be difficult to hide on the street, and there was the possibility that they would run into more CAGE recruits, but it was impossible to tell whether the alley offered escape or merely a dead end. Vergil glanced back through the doorway, seeing the goblins limping across the tavern toward them. They both seemed to have sustained minor injuries in the fall, which served to slow them down but—if the hateful looks on their faces were any indication—also to enrage them. They brandished curved swords of crude make that nevertheless looked more than capable of slicing a man's head off. Vergil began to doubt that these goblins intended to apprehend their prey without violence: these two had the appearance of overachievers.

"This way!" Vergil commanded, and made to turn left. But no sooner had he taken a step toward the street than a voice called from the darkness to their right, "Over here!"

Vergil hesitated, unsure whether the mysterious voice represented a trap or an unexpected ally. Apparently sensing his uncertainty, Handri took a step backwards, pressing his back against the door. Behind him, the door rattled as the goblins slammed into it. "Which way, sir?" he asked.

"Over here!" the voice on their right said again. "Quickly!"

Vergil peered into the darkness but could see nothing. He tried to make a rational assessment of their options: they could most likely outrun the two goblins, but if they ran into any resistance on the street, they were done for. They had no weapons, and Vergil was in no shape for a prolonged run through the city. Further, it could be argued that the principles of chivalry required Vergil to face the unknown lurker in the dark rather than flee. His aching muscles and joints concurred with chivalry.

"Change of tactics," Vergil announced, spinning on his heel. "This way!" He took off running into the shadows, moving as fast as his decrepit body would let him. The sound of footsteps on the pavement behind him confirmed that Handri was following. Almost immediately the alley was again flooded with light from inside the tavern as the door burst open and the goblins spilled into the alley, cursing and howling for blood.

When the door closed, Vergil found himself enveloped in darkness. He ran with his arms outstretched in front of him, expecting at any moment to trip over a dead dog or an old wagon wheel and go sprawling to the pavement, with Handri on top of him. The goblins, possessed of acute night vision, would likely be able to avoid any such hazards, and Vergil began to suspect he had made a serious tactical error. He slowed his pace.

"Keep going!" yelled the voice ahead of him in the dark. "Don't stop!"

Vergil gritted his teeth, closed his eyes, and put on a renewed burst of speed. This was no time for meekness: better to stumble in the dark and smash his teeth in than to be hamstrung by a goblin. At least that was what he was thinking when he ran headlong into something.

No, not something: *someone.* He felt arms wrap around his abdomen and a warm body give way, as if this person had been waiting to catch him. His momentum arrested somewhat, Vergil felt Handri slam into his back, and the three of them tumbled over each other in a chaotic mass of flailing limbs until Vergil found himself thrown free, landing with a thud on his back. He lay there with the wind knocked out of him, expecting at any moment to be done in either by the mysterious figure who had been lying in wait for him or, failing that, to be eviscerated by one of the two goblins coming up behind them. But the expected blow didn't come, and down the alley he heard two synchronized yelps followed by the sound of meat slamming against pavement.

"Get up," urged the voice, which he now realized belonged to a woman. A hand pulled at Vergil's sleeve.

"What... happened?" Vergil gasped, pulling himself to his feet with the stranger's help. To his left, he heard Handri getting to his feet as well. He peered down the alley, and against the light from the street he could just make out two figures lying prone several yards away. They were groaning and struggling to get to their feet.

"Tripwire," the stranger whispered. "Close your eyes and cover your ears."

"Close my..." Vergil murmured, unable to make sense of the command. There was a brief rustling sound next to him, followed by the sound of something hitting the pavement near the goblins. Vergil instinctively turned to look, connecting the sound with the stranger's command a split-second too late.

There was an incredibly loud *POP!*, like a cannonball striking a sheet of marble, accompanied by a flash brighter than lightning. Vergil clamped his eyes shut, but not before a bright red smear was painted across his field of vision. His ears rang from the sound. The goblins, who had received no warning, yelped in fear.

"Take this," said the stranger, and some kind of wire handle was thrust into Vergil's hand. The weight on the handle and the warmth on his hand told him it was a lantern, but nothing registered with his eyes. "Now, follow me." The stranger's voice was receding, but Vergil could still see nothing. He stumbled after the sound in the dark.

"Here, sir," said Handri's voice, as a leathery hand gripped his wrist. Handri took the handle from him while continuing to grip his wrist with his other hand. Handri pulled forward, and Vergil followed, trying to blink away the glare.

They jogged down the alley some distance and then made several turns in quick sequence before stopping abruptly. A sound like a door opening followed. "Duck, sir," said Handri, pulling him to the left. Still disoriented, it took Vergil a moment to realize that Handri wasn't pointing out the local waterfowl; smacking his head into a door jamb helped to clarify the matter. He recoiled, rubbing his head, and then hunched over and allowed himself to be led through the doorway. He followed Handri—who was presumably following the mysterious stranger—through a maze of narrow passageways. All around him, he heard unintelligible murmurs and whispers. Even in the dark, Vergil could sense that they had entered an entirely different part of the city. As they walked, Vergil became aware of a small glowing object bobbing like a drunken sparrow in front of him, occasionally disappearing altogether, and he realized after a few seconds that it was the flame of the lantern. Soon he could see Handri as well, or at least a garish caricature of him painted in yellowish light. Somewhere ahead of Handri, in the semi-darkness, a door opened, and the two of them followed the shadowy figure of the mysterious stranger through it into a dimly lit room. Vergil thought it odd that the stranger didn't also carry a light, but as he entered the room to see the stranger standing in front of him, he realized why.

"Good heavens!" Vergil exclaimed as he squinted at the small creature, still trying to clear the splotches from his vision. "You're a goblin!"

"And you are apparently not completely blind," said the goblin, "despite your inability to follow simple instructions." It took the lantern from Handri and hung it on a hook protruding from the ceiling.

As Vergil opened his mouth to respond, he realized he had seen this goblin somewhere before. "You were with the refugees the other night," he said.

"You have a gift for stating the obvious," said the goblin. "My name is Lagorna. I worked at the mill until you burned it down. My family is staying here with my sister until I can find work."

As Vergil's eyes adjusted to the dim light, he saw that several lumpy mattresses lay on the floor. He also realized that they were not alone. The doorway through which they had entered was crowded with goblins of various sizes trying to get a look at him and Handri. Distant whispers and murmurs indicated that many more goblins gathered just out of sight. "All right, no gawking," Lagorna snapped, waving her hands as if to shoo the goblins. "You've seen humans before." Disgruntled muttering followed, but one by one the goblin faces disappeared into the gloom.

"What is this place?" Vergil asked.

"This house is a communal residence owned by my sister and three other goblin families."

"But… What was that door we went through in the alley? What is this part of town?"

"Goblintown," said Lagorna. "It used to be a human neighborhood, but fifty years or so goblins began to move here in large numbers, and most of the humans left. Since then, the neighborhood has been walled off from the rest of the city, and most of the buildings have been connected with tunnels or covered passageways."

Vergil nodded. Even blind, he had felt the oppressive closeness as they made their way through the passages to this house. Now that he could see, he noticed the room was unnaturally dark—even considering that it was nighttime. He realized after a moment that all the windows in the place had been covered. He shuddered. "It feels like a cave," he said.

Lagorna smiled. "I'll pass the compliment along to my sister. She's worked very hard on the decor. You'll be safe here tonight."

Vergil frowned. "I assume you mean you'll keep us here until the morning, when you'll turn us over to CAGE."

"Well, that would be rather rude, wouldn't it?" Lagorna said. "Not to mention pointless. If I'd wanted CAGE to have you, I'd have let them have you. No, I mean you're welcome to stay as long as you want, but I would recommend leaving in the morning. The council knows better than to send its goons into Goblintown without permission, but I can't guarantee we can stall them forever."

"But… you're *goblins*," Vergil said. "Don't you want to kill us? Or see us thrown in a dungeon, at least?"

"This may surprise you," said Lagorna, "but it is possible not to hate someone simply for being different from you."

"I don't hate goblins for being different," said Vergil.

"Oh?" asked Lagorna. "Then why do you hate them?"

"Because *they* hate *us*!"

"There's no 'they,'" said Lagorna. "There's me and there's you. And I don't hate you. I'm a little irritated with you for burning down my place of employment, but I don't hate you."

"That was an accident," said Vergil.

"I know," said Lagorna. "That's why I'm only a little irritated. If I was extremely irritated, I wouldn't have saved you from those goons."

"Why *did* you save us?" asked Handri.

"I'm no fan of CAGE. They're creating more problems that they solve. Sending a bunch of thugs out to knock around anybody who's ever told an offensive goblin joke is not going to solve anything. Grimble should know better."

"You know Grimble?" asked Handri.

"We grew up together," said Lagorna. "We were in the same clan. He was always a bit of a firebrand; I wasn't surprised he went into politics, and I used to admire the way he stood up for the rights of goblins and other monsters. But lately something has changed. He's become mean-spirited and extreme in his methods. He seems to have lost sight of the goal of reconciling the different races of Dis; these days it's almost like he's fanning the flames of discord."

"So that's why you rescued us?" asked Vergil doubtfully. "Because you disapprove of Grimble's methods?"

"It's not the only reason," Lagorna admitted. "I felt I owed you, after you stood up to KLAMP."

"If I had not been there, KLAMP might not have bothered you in the first place. I was the one who emboldened them to confront you on the road."

"I realize that," said Lagorna, "but I could tell your heart was in the right place. You're a little dim, but you're not a hateful man."

Vergil frowned, wondering if it was true. He *did* still hate goblins, didn't he? The bad ones, anyway. He supposed it was possible there were a few good ones—like Lagorna, if indeed this wasn't some sort of trick to lure them into the clutches of the KLAMP. But if it were, she certainly put a lot of effort into making their escape look convincing.

"Anyway," Lagorna went on, "don't trip over yourselves thanking me. I can only spare this room for a night. After that, I consider us even."

"Your hospitality is much appreciated," Vergil said, a bit embarrassed that he had to be reminded of basic courtesy by a goblin.

"But what will we do?" asked Handri. "We have no money, and no place to go. We can't run from CAGE forever."

Lagorna shrugged. "If I were you, I'd hop the first freight train out of town. If you're not up for fleeing, I'd suggest throwing yourself on the mercy of the council. Now that CAGE is after you, they're not going to stop. Are you hungry?"

"Famished," said Handri.

Vergil felt a gnawing in his stomach but, knowing what qualified as 'food' for goblins, was reluctant to say anything.

"I don't suppose you'll trust any meat I give you," said Lagorna, as if reading his mind. "But I think I can find some bread and vegetables. We've already eaten, so I will bring the food to you."

"That would be wonderful," said Handri.

"Bread and vegetables would be welcome sustenance," said Vergil. "And perhaps some beer, if you have it."

"I think I can scare some up," said Lagorna. "We aren't completely uncivilized, after all." She turned and left the room, returning a few minutes later with a platter of food. Trailing behind her was the young goblin who had been with her the night they had met on the road. He held a mug of beer in each hand. Lagorna set the platter on one of the mattresses while the little goblin hung back in the doorway, regarding Vergil nervously.

"Come now, Delmer," said Lagorna. "They're just humans. They won't bite."

Delmer shuffled into the room, handing one mug to Handri, and then the other to Vergil.

"Thank you, young man," said Vergil, not realizing what he'd said until the words had left his mouth. The young goblin grinned sheepishly and then turned and ran out of the room."

"Delmer's a little bashful," said Lagorna. "He's been that way since his father died."

"I am... sorry to hear that," said Vergil.

Lagorna shrugged. "It's one reason I'm not terribly broken up about the loss of the mill. The money was good, relatively speaking, but it was a dangerous place to work. Delmer's father fell into one of the machines, and was killed almost instantly. In a way, he was lucky, I suppose. Many times the worker survives, but loses an arm or a leg. It's hard enough for a goblin to find work these days, and a goblin missing a limb has almost no chance. Not that we let any of our own starve, of course. The one thing goblins have going for us is our fierce loyalty to our clans."

Vergil nodded, thinking this over. He'd never considered before how hard it must be to be a goblin in a land dominated by humans. And he'd always thought of goblins' clan loyalty as evidence of their mindless, collective affinity for large-scale destruction, but these days at least it seemed it was mostly a survival mechanism. Maybe it had always been so. In a way, Vergil thought, goblins have their own code of chivalry that is every bit as rigorous, admirable and impractical as mine.

"I will leave you to eat in peace," Lagorna said as Vergil and Handri sat down on either side of the platter. "It's late, so I would suggest bedding down once you have eaten. Chamber pot is in the corner; I'm afraid indoor plumbing is still something of a novelty in Goblintown."

"Much obliged," said Vergil. Lagorna bowed and left the room, closing the door behind her.

Vergil didn't had to be reminded of the lateness of the hour. Once he had eaten enough to take the edge off his hunger, he drifted to sleep.

Twelve

Vergil awoke the next morning with a clear—if not particularly welcome—idea of what he must do. It was time to face the consequences of his actions: the burning of the mill, the confrontation with the refugees, his testimony in front of the city council. The city had been seized by fear, and it was largely his fault. Having started out with the best of intentions, he had nevertheless somehow been reduced to fleeing through alleyways and cowering in a goblin lair, and nothing good would come of continuing on this path. If taking responsibility for his actions resulted in him being thrown in a dungeon—or even hanged in the city square—so be it. He had already lived a longer life than probably any other human in Dis, and although he had spent most of it in bed, he supposed the universe didn't owe him any more time. Further, it seemed that all of his dearly held principles and prejudices were now worse than worthless; he was a walking catastrophe, a danger to all those around him. Already he had probably ruined Handri's life; it would have been better for them both if Vergil had been able to sleep through his gradual dismemberment: it might have bought Handri a few more months of relative happiness at his estate. He pledged that he would plead for lenience toward Handri, even at the expense of tarnishing his own name. Chivalry be damned; he would not cause poor Handri any more trouble if he could manage it.

For now, Handri remained untroubled in sleep, and Vergil intended to leave him that way. Hopefully by the time he awoke, Vergil would have resolved their fugitive status one way or another. He got quietly out of bed and tiptoed to the door. Beyond it, he heard a buzz of activity: the sounds of cooking and other chores being undertaken along with a constant drone of conversation punctuated by the occasional playful shout or gentle scolding. It reminded him of the bustling estate where he had grown up, and he wondered if the simple joys of childhood were as wasted on these young goblins as they had been on him.

He stepped into the hall, closing the door quietly behind him. Enough daylight filtered through the partially blocked windows that he had little trouble finding his way down the hall, past the various rooms filled with young goblins playing games and older goblins reading or engaged in various chores, from darning socks to churning butter. Most of the adult goblins seemed to be female—evidently it was more common for males to work outside of the den—but there were several males as well. Many of the adults—both male and female—were missing one or more limbs, and many more had visible scars or other deformities. Vergil resisted the urge to shudder as he walked past. The goblins, for their part, studiously ignored him, except for the occasional curious child. He didn't see Lagorna or any other goblins he recognized. He made it to the front door without incident.

The door opened into a tunnel-like corridor built of scraps of wood, metal and canvas, and lit only by sunlight streaming through the occasional crack. It meandered left and right, occasionally breaking off into smaller avenues, and Vergil began to wonder if he should have tried to locate Lagorna and asked her for a guide to help him find his way out of Goblintown. Several times he was passed by goblins hurrying past him one direction or another, but they paid him no heed. Vergil found the dark, confined passage discomfiting. The goblins rushing by, along with the buzz of activity going on unseen nearby, only heightened the feeling. He stopped to rest a moment at an intersection and found that he had no idea which direction he had come from or where he was supposed to be going. The walls seemed to be closing in on him, and he was suddenly short of breath. He staggered toward the wall and tried to brace himself, but his hand hit a patch of canvass that gave way beneath his fingertips. He fell to his knees as the passageway spun around him.

"Sir, are you alright?" a small voice behind him asked.

"Eh?" asked Vergil, on his hands and knees. "I'm fine." He forced himself to breathe deeply and affix his eyes on a stationary point of light in the far wall.

"You sure?" said the voice. "You don't look fine."

"Look," snapped Vergil, "this is none of your—" He glanced behind him to see a small female goblin, even younger than Lagorna's son, staring at him. Even in the dim light, the concern on the child's face was evident. Vergil sighed. "I will be all right," he said. "I just got a little…"

"Scared?" said the girl.

Vergil had been about to say "dizzy," but at this point there seemed to be no point in trying to maintain face. And the fact was, he *had* been scared. Chivalry frowned on such an admission, but he realized now that he'd been scared ever since he woke up from his slumber—and maybe some time before that. Scared of monsters, scared of getting old, and, above all, scared of change. "There just doesn't seem to be any correct move," he found himself saying.

"That's easy," said the girl. "Follow the hands."

For a moment, Vergil couldn't connect the girl's words to anything. Then he realized he was talking about getting out of the maze. "Hands?" he asked.

"Sure," said the girl, walking to the wall. He pointed at a faded blue goblin hand print on the wall. Vergil saw now that there was one every ten feet or so. He hadn't noticed them before in the dim light. "Blue takes you back to the human city."

"The human city," Vergil repeated. The words sounded strange to him. For all his doubts about the practicality of multiple races living together in a single community, it never occurred to him that monsters still considered Avaressa a "human city." Did they feel as out of place there as he did in these makeshift passageways?

Vergil struggled to his feet, and the girl did his best to help him. The dizziness seemed to have passed. He felt like he should give the girl something for his trouble, but he had left Handri with the money. "Thank you," he said.

"You're welcome, sir," said the girl with a smile. She turned and ran off down one of the side passages.

Vergil sighed and began to trudge toward the exit. It was becoming more and more difficult for him to maintain the purity of his hatred toward goblins. He had begrudgingly accepted that there existed a few exceptions to the rule that goblins were universally vile and rapacious, but as he encountered more of them, he was having a hard time resisting the idea that there was as wide a range in the attitudes and inclinations among goblins as there was among humans. With the exception of Handri, in fact, he had received better treatment from goblins since waking from his long sleep than from his own kind. Possibly this was a result of the debasement of the human race over the past century, but was it not just as likely that goblins had become more civilized during his slumber? Or had the supposed differences between the two races been an illusion to begin with? This proposition seemed dubious, but he hoped it was true, as he would soon be throwing himself on the mercy of the council, whose goblin members seemed to have an inordinate amount of power.

Eventually Vergil found himself in front of a small wooden door in a brick wall. He took it for the same door that he and Handri had come through the previous night, but once he went through it he realized he was in a completely different alley. After meandering through alleys and streets for some time, he managed to get his bearings and made his way toward the city council chambers. Things seemed to have settled down a bit in the city, although it was just after dawn so probably not many troublemakers—of either KLAMP- or CAGE-persuasion—were out and about yet. Vergil was acutely self-conscious as he walked down the street, expecting at any moment to be waylaid by a gang of goblins, but so far the only goblins he saw were too busy sweeping sidewalks, carting bags of flour, or engaged in various other productive activities to take any notice of him. In any case, he was fairly certain that creeping furtively through the shadows to the council building would only draw more attention. Better to walk boldly down the middle of the street and hope that anybody looking for him would assume he wouldn't be so unabashed about being seen.

This plan went awry, though, when he nearly walked headlong into a well-dressed man exiting a carriage parked in front of the council building. He'd been so intent on appearing nonchalant that he'd been oblivious to his surroundings. As he opened his mouth to apologize, he realized that he recognized this man: it was Thameril, the mayor himself. Thameril hadn't yet seen Vergil, as he had turned to speak to someone still in the carriage. Vergil halted and stepped backwards, ducking behind it.

"—stirring up all sorts of trouble," someone in the carriage was saying. "My boss doesn't want him running his mouth off all over town." The voice seemed familiar to Vergil, but he couldn't at first place it.

"But what choice do we have?" said Thameril. "He's something of a local celebrity, you know. Frankly, I think it's just as well he got away last night. If he'd been thrown in the dungeon—or worse, been killed—the backlash would be—"

"I understand your concerns," the man in the carriage said. "But Grimble feels it is better to deal with him now than after he's built a coalition against us." Recognition dawned on Vergil: the voice of the man in the carriage belonged to Bander, the council messenger who had come to urge him to testify against KLAMP. Did he secretly work for Grimble?

"Do we even have any indication that is his plan?" Thameril asked. "I don't see anyone rallying to his cause. So far, all he has done is talk, and his remarks have been fairly tame. The situation in the city is already bad, what with your boss's goons running around scaring the daylights out of people. If we start preemptively imprisoning people, we're going to create the opposition he's trying to prevent."

"You propose we wait until the threat is more severe before we act?" Bander said. "That's foolishness, Thameril. The matter has been decided. Don't forget your arrangement with Grimble. The truth about your dealings with those idiot vigilantes could still come out."

"Fine," Thameril said curtly. "We'll do it your way, but don't say I didn't warn you. Do you know where he is?"

"He shouldn't be difficult to find," said Bander, "particularly if he's still with that fool henchman of his. We'll send a horde of CAGE goblins to bring them in."

"I hope your boss knows what he's doing," Thameril replied.

"Good day, Thameril." Bander barked a command at the driver, and the carriage pulled away from the curb. Vergil, finding himself suddenly with no place to hide, spun around and did his best to walk surreptitiously away from Thameril. Fortunately, Thameril made a beeline for the council building, taking no notice of him. Vergil stood across the street watching him and wondered what he was going to do now. It seemed that the council was not currently in session, and in any case it was probably pointless to request an audience with them now. Grimble had already decided he was a threat, to be eliminated at the first opportunity, and he had corrupted Thameril as well. If Vergil couldn't even rely on the humans on the council to be impartial, what chance did he have? Vergil was all for facing his circumstances head on, but going to the council now would be suicidal—particularly now that Vergil knew of Grimble's vendetta against him. Had Grimble instructed Bander to warn Vergil about the KLAMP and coach him in his testimony? Feeling baffled and overwhelmed, Vergil darted into an alley where he could assess his options.

Fleeing town was the coward's way out, and if he didn't find some way to make some money, he wouldn't make it very far in any case. The only alternative, though, was to stay and make a stand against CAGE, but he wasn't sure how to go about doing that. To effectively resist the abuses of CAGE, it seemed that he would somehow have to do exactly what Thameril and Grimble feared he would do: rally people to his cause by convincing them that the council had gone too far in its efforts to stamp out anti-goblin sentiment. The obvious problem with this idea was that Vergil would have a hard time living down his reputation as a goblin-hater. Everyone would naturally assume that he was railing against CAGE because of his own prejudices. Even if he were to completely renounce his anti-goblin bias—which, admittedly, he was not quite ready to do in any case—any action he took would be tainted by suspicion of bigotry. If he were more adept with current idioms and customs, he might have a chance of convincing people his heart was in the right place, but whenever he attempted to clarify his thoughts, he seemed to make things worse.

What he need, he realized, was an ally. And unfortunately there was only one possible candidate for the position: Marko, Lord Balphry himself. He cursed himself for not cooperating when Marko had approached him. Yes, Marko had bilked him out of his investments, but it had been childish pique that had prompted him to reject Marko's request for assistance. The one time relying on his chivalric principles might actually have benefited him, and he had acted out of spite instead. And now he would have to go to Marko, hat in hand, and hope that his offer of cooperation was still open.

Now that he knew that Grimble was going to be sending his goons with specific instructions to capture him, Vergil decided it behooved him to be a little stealthier in his movements. Marko's apartment was only a few blocks from here, but it wouldn't do to run into CAGE agents on the way over. So he skirted the main streets, keeping to the side streets and alleys, zigzagging in the general direction of the apartment. It occurred to him that Grimble might be aware that Vergil and Handri had been staying at Marko's apartment, but the possibility of running into CAGE agents at the apartment was a risk he was going to have to take.

Vergil exited an alley just down the street and across from the apartment. Pausing to take a look around, he saw that the street was quiet. No activity was evident in the apartment, but he would just have to hope that Marko was there. He made a beeline across the street toward the front door of the building. He was only a few paces away when a rough-looking goblin with a patch over his left eye came around the corner and stopped a few steps away, looking directly at him. Two more goblins, both with swords at their sides, were right behind the first one. Vergil realized with sudden horror that he recognized these two: they were both bandaged and limping from being thrown out the window by Yurgi the day before. One of them had bandages covering most of his face covering wounds acquired from colliding with the pavement.

Vergil froze. The honorable thing to do would be to stand and fight, but he had no weapon and was no match for four goblins in any case. He was determined not to run, so he did the only thing he could do. He raised his hands in surrender.

Thirteen

"You!" growled the goblin with the eye patch, wagging his finger at Vergil. "Get lost!"

Vergil blinked at the goblin uncomprehendingly, while the other two continued to glare at him. The expressions on their face—particularly the one whose face was almost entirely concealed by bandages—were unreadable. As they stood there, several more goblins spilled around the corner.

"I said scram!" the goblin in the lead snapped. "This is official CAGE business!"

Vergil slowly put down his hands and backed away. The two wounded goblins looked at each other and shrugged. When Vergil retreated, the leader returned wrangling the other goblins, who continued to pour around the corner. There were now at least a dozen, and two of them were carrying a long, heavy pipe with handles: a battering ram. The other goblins moved out of the way and those carrying the ram rushed the front door of the building, sending it flying open with a crash. They ran with the ram up the stairs, the rest of the party disappearing after them. Another crash soon followed, and the shouts from the upstairs window told Vergil that Marko was indeed home. The low, terrifying growl of an ogre told him that Marko was not alone.

It was difficult to make sense of the fracas that followed. Goblin battle cries were difficult to distinguish from goblin screams of terror. At one point, two goblins were ejected from the window in quick sequence, landing with a crunch at Vergil's feet. It was difficult to be certain, given their condition, but Vergil thought they were the same two goblins who had been thrown out the window the day before. This time, though, they had missed the refuse pile by a few inches, and it didn't look like they would be getting up again.

Eventually the noise from the apartment died down. Vergil heard the sound of footsteps coming down the steps, and he backed away so as to be less conspicuous. The goblins, many of them bloody or limping, came down the stairs, one by one. One of the last few was prodding Marko, bruised and disheveled, his hands tied in front of him, ahead of him with his sword. A few of the others picked up their dead companions and carried them away. Vergil needn't have worried about being seen; the goblins continued to take no notice of him. They disappeared back around the corner, prodding Marko ahead of them. Marko was too dazed and frightened to take any notice of Vergil. There was no sign of Yurgi the ogress.

As the caravan disappeared from view, Vergil cursed his vanity and foolishness. It wasn't Vergil that Grimble and Thameril were worried about; it was Marko! So fixated was he on his own plight that Vergil had assumed the conspirators could only be talking about him. But of course Vergil had done nothing worthy of concern on the part of the council or CAGE; all he'd done is make a few ill-advised comments in a tavern. And the "fool henchman" was not Handri, but rather the ogress, Yurgi.

Whatever relief Vergil felt at escaping capture was outweighed by his embarrassment. Marko had even told him he intended to "manage things" himself. Vergil should have understood that this meant organizing resistance to CAGE. While Vergil was making a fool of himself in the local tavern, Marko was doing what he could to suppress the insanity that had taken over the city. Whatever his personal feelings toward Marko, he had to admit that was a laudable goal. If Vergil hadn't been so pigheaded, he might have been able to help Marko achieve it. But now Marko was in the hands of CAGE, and the insanity would continue to spread.

The good news was that Vergil's own offenses apparently did not warrant much attention. The two goblins who had pursued him down the alley the previous night—and who were now deceased— had showed little interest in him, and the leader had been completely oblivious. If any general notice had gone out to the CAGE membership about the importance of his capture, surely the two injured goblins would have alerted the leader, but they had said nothing. In the scheme of things, Vergil was just a minor annoyance; the real threat, in Grimble's eyes, was Marko.

When the goblins were out of sight, Vergil ran across the street and up the stairs to the apartment. He found a bruised and bloody Yurgi, lying on the floor clutching her right leg and grimacing in pain. She glared suspiciously at Vergil as he entered, but he held up his hands to signal that he intended her no harm.

"Are you with *them*?" Yurgi asked anxiously. "Where did they take Lord Balphry?"

"I am not with the goblins, no," said Vergil. "That is, the goblins who attacked you." He wasn't sure why he felt the need to clarify this. "What did they do to you?"

"Smashed my knee with that ram," Yurgi moaned. "Caught me off guard."

"You may need a splint," Vergil said. "If you allow me to inspect the injury—"

"Forget about me!" Yurgi yelped. "If you want to help, help my boss! Go get those goblins!"

"Yurgi," said Vergil, "There is little I can do for Lord Balphry in my current state, and your injury—"

"Please!" Yurgi yelped. "I don't know what I'll do without him!" The ogress appeared on the verge of tears.

Vergil hesitated, a bit taken aback by Yurgi's expression of emotion. He had assumed she was merely a hired thug, but it seemed that Yurgi had a serious attachment to Marko. Vergil glanced out the side window and saw the goblin gang marching Marko down the street. Thanks to their wounded—and dead—members, they weren't moving very quickly.

"Do you see him?" Yurgi asked desperately.

"Yes, but—"

"Please, go help him!"

Vergil studied the ogre, then glanced out the window again at the slow-moving procession. He might not be able to stop them—and didn't feel particularly inclined to risk his neck for Marko in any case—but he supposed he could tail them to their destination. He could then inform Yurgi where her boss had been taken, which seemed the least he could do under the circumstances.

Well, no, he thought. The *least* he could do would be to forget the whole business with CAGE and go have a beer. After all, apparently Grimble wasn't out to get him after all, and the two goblins who had a solid reason to have a grudge against him were dead. He had no compelling rationale to involve himself any further in the internal politics of Avaressa.

And yet, regarding Yurgi lying on the floor of the apartment clutching her smashed knee and blubbering about her beloved boss, Vergil couldn't help feeling…what? Sympathy? Guilt? Either sentiment was nigh indefensible. Yurgi was an ogre, for Grovlik's sake! Ogres were monsters, notorious for waylaying unsuspecting travelers and plucking infants from their cribs—not that Yurgi seemed to be the sort to do the latter. A knight worthy of the title would gladly die rather than do the bidding of an ogre. And yet, Vergil could not escape his responsibility for Marko's capture. If he had done his chivalric duty by coming to a fellow aristocrat's aid when asked, Marko would not currently be on his way to some dank dungeon, and a toga-clad ogre would not be whimpering on the rug before him. Vergil sighed.

"Wait here," he said, for no reason other than that it seemed to be the thing to say. "I will attempt a reconnaissance mission."

Yurgi nodded, and a weak smile appeared on her face.

Vergil turned and ran back down the stairs, intent on catching the goblin gang while he still could. He caught up with them a block or so away and followed them for some time. Occasionally other pedestrians would stop and stare, murmuring worriedly to each other, obviously having recognized Lord Balphry. Marko, for his part, kept his face downcast and did his best not to be seen. This was clearly a mortifying experience for him. Fortunately, the procession made for such a spectacle that Vergil remained completely unnoticed following thirty or so paces behind them.

At one point a well-dressed couple crossed the street in front of the gang, the gentleman doing his best to pretend not to see the goings-on. But his wife, a heavyset woman in a powder blue dress, stopped dead in the middle of the street, staring open-mouthed at the goblins.

"Come, dear," the husband murmured, tugging at her arm. He was a slightly built, nervous-looking man with slicked-back hair and a pencil mustache.

But the woman was having none of it. "Marko!" she cried in a shrill voice, drawing the attention of everyone on the street who wasn't already watching. "What have they done to you?"

Before Marko could make any kind of reply, the goblin with the eyepatch stepped in front of him. "Official CAGE business, ma'am. Out of the way!"

"CAGE?" asked the woman, astounded. "What in Dis is *CAGE*?"

"It's the new goblin equality committee," said her husband, still averting his eyes. "We received a notice about it this morning. It's none of our concern."

"But that's Marko! Hello, Marko!" she called, craning her head to peer around the goblin leader.

"Step aside, ma'am," the goblin with the eye patch said.

"You can't talk to me like that," said the woman. "What are you doing with Marko? I demand you release him at once!"

"We don't take orders from your kind," snapped the goblin, losing his composure. "Now get out of the way!"

"My *kind*?" asked the woman. "Why, you're just a... a thug!"

The goblin snarled and drew his sword, advancing toward the woman. She was a good two feet taller than he, but neither of the humans were armed, and Vergil knew that goblins were fierce fighters despite their size. Why, this group of a dozen had managed to overpower an ogre! Even if Yurgi had been surprised, that was no small feat.

The husband, to his credit, stepped in front of his wife and puffed out his chest in an attempt to look threatening. "See here, friend," he said. "We're all for goblin rights and whatnot, but it's unseemly to march a respected member of the aristocracy down the street in this manner. What are the charges against Lord Balphry?"

The goblin spat. "I ain't your friend," he growled, bringing the tip of his sword within an inch of the man's throat. "And in my book, being human is crime enough. You look pretty guilty to me."

"This is absurd!" the man yelped, his voice quavering. "You'll never get away with this."

Vergil had crept up to within a few paces of the gang, and was deliberating whether to intercede. He wouldn't have any better luck in a fight with the goblins, but he might at least distract them long enough for the couple to get away.

But with a sword at her husband's throat, the woman seemed to suddenly grasp the seriousness of the situation. "It's all right, Laris," she said quietly, putting her hand on his shoulder. "It's none of our business."

The man glared at the goblin for a moment, but then turned away. He took his wife's arm and they moved quickly away. The leader bared his teeth in a ghastly grin and sheathed his sword. Vergil breathed a sigh of relief.

"Let's go, men," the leader growled, and the procession continued again. Two of the goblins were carrying deceased comrades over their shoulders and looked ready to collapse. Vergil suspected they couldn't be going much farther.

He was right. The procession soon turned down a street toward a wealthier neighborhood, finally stopping in front of a gate in a brick wall that encircled a large house set back from the road a hundred yards or so, atop a large hill. In Vergil's day, this part of the city was still unsettled; the land was too rocky and hilly to farm and the aristocrats tended to live on estates like Vergil's farther outside the city. Those that lived in town tended to have apartments closer to the center of the city, like the one Vergil had just come from. Evidently the city's new aristocrats, who had become wealthy from manufacturing and other capitalistic endeavors, had decided it was worth the effort to clear the land and build fancy new houses within walking distance of the city proper.

After some negotiations between the goblin leader and an attendant at the gate, the gate swung open and the goblins swarmed through. Vergil crossed the street toward the wall as he watched the goblins march up the walk toward the imposing residence. There was no way he was going to get through that gate, but the wall was barely taller than he was; it seemed designed more to appear foreboding than to actually stop anyone from getting through.

The sensible thing to do at this point would be to return to the apartment, tell Yurgi where Marko was, and let her do what she liked with the information. But he found himself overwhelmed with curiosity. He had expected Marko to be brought to a prison or dungeon, not to a private residence. Who lived here?

He walked along the street, pausing to smile and bow at a pair of young women walking the other way. When he reached the corner, he ducked around it, and trotted along the wall until found a small boulder. He rolled this toward the base of the wall, stepped on top of it, and gripped the top of the wall with his fingers. It was all he could do to force his tired muscles to pull himself onto the top of the wall, and for a moment he lay there trembling and sweating. He was some distance from the gate, but he would be hard to miss if the attendant happened to look in his direction. In an effort to climb quickly down the other side, he lost his grip and fell awkwardly into the shrubbery.

Tired and scratched up but otherwise uninjured, he managed with some difficulty to extricate himself from the bushes. He crouched for a moment between the shrubs and the wall, peering over the top of the branches toward the house. The goblins had made their way to the front door. After a moment, the door opened and an animated exchange occurred between the goblin leader and someone inside the house. They seemed to come to some kind of agreement, and then the door opened and the leader prodded Marko inside with his sword. The leader spoke briefly again with the figure inside the house—from where Vergil stood, he couldn't tell if it was a human or a goblin—and then stepped back on the porch, leaving Marko inside. The door slammed shut behind him. A momentary quarrel erupted between the goblins, climaxing with the leader telling the group to shut their "filthy gobs" and follow him. He marched back down the sidewalk and the others followed, moaning and grumbling. The two carrying their deceased fellows looked to be near collapse.

Once the goblins began to file out of the gate and the human attendant was preoccupied with getting them out, Vergil jogged across the lush green lawn toward the house and then pressed himself up against the wall, out of the gate attendant's view. Seeing nothing of interest in the first window he came to, he moved along the side of the house, peeking in each window as he passed. The third window looked into a drawing room, where he saw Marko tied to a chair. Closer to the window, with his back to Vergil, was a goblin. Vergil recognized him by the long staff he held in his right hand: Grimble. There was no one else in the room. Grimble was talking, but Vergil couldn't make out what he was saying through the window. The stolid expression on Marko's face, along with the way Grimble was gesticulating in agitation told him that Grimble was trying to convince Marko of something—without much success. This went on for several minutes, with Marko grimly shaking his head, and Grimble growing more and more animated. At last, Grimble seemed to give up. He turned and walked a few steps toward the window, and for a moment Vergil thought Grimble had seen him. But Grimble was clearly preoccupied, his eyes unfocused and staring straight ahead. He stopped and closed his eyes, spreading his arms slightly. What was Grimble doing? Vergil wondered. Meditating?

But as Vergil watched, he noticed a strange shimmer in the air around Grimble. Vergil blinked several times, but the shimmer continued to intensify, and a glance at Marko confirmed that he saw it as well. Something very strange was happening to Grimble. The shimmer seemed to spread out from Grimble but also up, until it reached almost to the ceiling. Soon the figure of Grimble was blotted out entirely by the aura, which had become so bright that Vergil had to squint to continue looking at it. But just as quickly the intensity began to fade, and in its place was the figure of a man— thin and slightly hunched over, but still a good three feet taller than Grimble. As the shimmer continued to fade, Vergil saw that the man was fairly old, and was wearing a long, dark blue robe. Grimble had simply vanished and been replaced by this man. Vergil was so astounded at the transformation that he didn't at first notice that the man now really was looking right at him. Vergil's daze was only shattered when the man pointed directly at him and began shouting. From somewhere upstairs, Vergil heard the pounding of footsteps.

Fourteen

Vergil turned and broke into an ambling run. His joints had stiffened up even more when he fell, and standing stock still at the window for several minutes hadn't helped any. He didn't know who Grimble had summoned, but he had no doubt whoever it was could outrun him. His only hope was to get to—and over—the wall before they grabbed him. Pain shot through his knees with every step, and soon he was gasping for breath. Risking a glance over his shoulder, he caught sight of four goblins, dressed in black uniforms, coming around the rear of the house toward him. He was almost halfway to the wall.

The rush of hope he felt at the possibility of making it to the wall was immediately dampened when he realized he had nothing to stand on to get over it. He hadn't planned on having to make an emergency exit, and he found himself looking around frantically for a bucket or planter to move against the base of the wall. He saw no suitable candidate, and the shrubs and other small plants near the wall would never bear his weight. The only thing to do was to attempt to vault over the wall without slowing down. The odds of him doing this successfully were slim, and he would likely break a few bones in the attempt. Even if he somehow made it over the wall in one piece, the goblins—who would have no trouble scaling the bricks with their clawed fingers and toes—would be right behind him. But the alternative was certain capture, after which he would be dragged back to the house, where he would share whatever horrible fate Grimble (or whoever it was he had seen in the house) had planned for Marko.

As he neared the wall, he extended his right leg, planting the sole of his right shoe against the wall. Ignoring the screaming in his knee, he allowed his momentum to carry him forward and up, managing to hook his fingertips on the top edge. Without slowing, he pulled himself up, straining to get his arms and shoulders on top of the wall. Momentum only got him halfway, though, and he found himself shakily struggling to pull himself the rest of the way up. He had neither the time nor the strength for a second try; if his arms gave out, he would fall into the clutches of the goblins. Below him, he heard snarls and shouts, and the thought of the little monsters' foul teeth sinking into his flesh gave him a burst of strength—just enough to get his upper body on top of the wall. Goblins clutched at his feet, but he kept moving, rolling over the top and bracing for a fall on the other side. The ground here was a good seven feet down, and he had little hope of surviving the impact with his bones intact. But in the split second that he teetered on the top of the wall, he caught sight of an oak sapling a few paces away. Managing to get his right foot underneath him before he toppled off the wall, he pushed off, flailing awkwardly toward the tree. He crashed into the upper branches, desperately trying to get a grip on something as he fell. At last he got his right hand around a limb the thickness of his thumb and held on tightly, the little tree bending from his weight. He sailed in a broad arc toward the ground, his momentum gradually slowing. Just as his fingers began to slip, his toes gently touched the ground. He looked up to see one of the four goblins perched on top of the wall, dagger raised, about to leap down on top of Vergil. Another goblin was climbing up behind the first.

The branch slipped from his fingers and the tree sprang back to vertical—and then a few degrees past vertical, just enough to smack the goblin square in the face. He stood for a moment at the top of the wall, dazed, then dropped his dagger and fell backwards on top of the goblin behind him. There was a thud as the goblins landed on the ground, and then the sounds of groans and cursing.

Vergil didn't stick around to see how quickly the goblins could get back up the wall; he turned and ran through the woods, the trees soon giving way to another residential street. This was an older neighborhood where the houses were smaller and closer together.

Vergil turned right and loped down the road, looking desperately for some place to hide. He couldn't keep running much longer, and already he could hear the goblins crashing through the trees behind him. He was exhausted and out of breath, and his knees felt like they were going to give out at any moment.

Stopping to get his breath at the mouth of an alley, he spotted a bicycle leaning against the back of a house. It was much smaller than the one he had ridden before, but this was clearly his only possible means of escape. His old bones wouldn't let him run any farther, and there was no place to hide. Behind him, the goblins shouted as they exited the woods and spotted him.

Vergil hobbled down the alley, gasping for breath and leaning against the wall of the house to steady himself. He reached the bicycle just as the goblins came around the corner. They cursed at him as he stood the bicycle up and straddled it, placing his right foot on the pedal and pushing off with his left. The bicycle wobbled and careened wildly, first to the left and then to the right. Vergil peddled furiously, his knees nearly colliding with his chin at the top of their arc. Too afraid and preoccupied to look back, Vergil could hear the shouts and curses of the goblins only a few steps behind him. He was riding not much faster than he could walk; twice he felt a goblin snatching at the back of his shirt, but his erratic movements made it impossible for them to anticipate where he would be, and both times he slipped free. After leading the furious goblins past seven or eight houses, Vergil started to get the hang of the bicycle and managed to push his legs hard enough to put on a little more speed. As he sailed down the street, he risked a glance back and saw the three goblins standing together, panting and cursing. One of them waved its fist at him.

To be sure he was safe, Vergil rode for nearly another mile before stopping. He had a brief moment of panic when he realized this bicycle had no brakes—or if it did, they were not on the handlebars where he expected them to be. Pressing the only lever on the handlebars resulted in a pleasant but not particularly helpful tinkling sound. Fortunately he had come upon a relatively undeveloped area of the city; thick weeds grew on either side of the road, and to the right the shoulder sloped down to a shallow ditch. He steered the bike off the road, the weeds whipping at his bare feet. Gradually the bike slowed and he tumbled gently to the ground at the bottom of the ditch. He staggered away from the bike and fell to his knees, then toppled over and lay moaning on the ground, overwhelmed with pain and exhaustion. His entire body hurt. He could only hope he was hidden well enough that any CAGE goons who happened by wouldn't see him, because he was in no shape to flee any farther.

At some point he must have fallen asleep, because he was awakened by someone standing over him and yelling. He was seized with fear, thinking the goblins had caught up to him—but the face hanging over him, ugly though it was, belonged to a human: Handri.

"—not safe for you to be sleeping here!" Handri was shouting. "Please, sir, get up!"

Vergil groaned and pulled himself into a sitting position. Judging by the angle of the sun, he'd been out for several hours. He blinked dumbly in the light, trying to remember how he had gotten there and what he had intended to do next.

"Why did you leave, sir? I've been looking all over for you. Lagorna said you left without a word. I finally thought to go to Lord Balphry's apartment. Yurgi said that a gang of goblins surprised them and dragged Lord Balphry off, and you went after them. A woman I ran into down the street said she saw an old man lying on the grass next to this road, but she was unable to awaken you. I thought you had fallen into a coma again. Or worse."

"Nay, Handri," said Vergil. "I simply had a bit too much excitement for a man my age. Give me a hand, would you?" With Handri's help, Vergil got to his feet. His muscles and joints were so sore that he wasn't sure he could walk. "How far are we from Marko's apartment?" he asked.

"Maybe half a mile," said Handri. "What is going on, sir?"

Vergil sighed. "I wish I knew. For now, I need to get back to Marko's apartment and tell Yurgi what happened to Marko. Is there a way we can get there without walking?"

"I can try to flag down a cab," said Handri. "Will you be alright a moment?"

Vergil was leaning heavily on Handri, but he nodded and managed to stand on his own. Handri took off running, disappearing around a corner of a busier street. Vergil was about to fall over when he caught sight of a carriage coming down the street toward him. Handri hopped out and helped him inside, and then gave the driver directions to Marko's apartment. Vergil leaned back against the cushioned seat of the carriage and felt himself drifting back to unconsciousness.

"Sir!" Handri cried. "You can't go to sleep yet. You have to tell me what happened."

"To be perfectly honest," said Vergil, "I cannot be certain. My most cherished beliefs have been revealed to be falsehoods, and now I cannot even trust my own eyes!" He proceeded to tell Handri of the day's adventures, including his vision of Grimble transforming into the strange robed man. Handri listened in silence, and when Vergil finished, he rubbed his chin thoughtfully.

"I have gone mad, haven't I?" asked Vergil. "Why, I have probably imagined everything that has happened since I woke up. Good heavens, Vergil. What if I never even woke up?"

"You woke up, sir," Handri assured him. "I was there, remember?"

"Yes, but..." Vergil started. He wasn't sure how Handri would take the news that he existed only in Vergil's imagination. Vergil supposed he would not take it well.

"What is it, sir?"

"Nothing, Handri. I am just beginning to despair of ever making sense of this world."

"Oh," said Handri. "That's too bad."

Vergil frowned. This wasn't the response he had expected. "What do you mean, it's too bad?" he asked. "I am in the thralls of an existential crisis, and all you have to say is that it's too bad?"

"I just meant that it's too bad you're giving up making sense of the world, because I think I just figured out one small thing myself, and I had intended to share my thought with you in the hopes that it might fit into some larger scheme that you could then explain to me."

"I see," said Vergil dubiously. "And what is this thought of yours?"

"Well," said Handri uncertainly, "it seems that this man who has been posing as Grimble is capable of creating powerful illusions."

"Yes," said Vergil. "And?"

"And didn't you say that Grimble told the council that the goblins who stole the zelaznium were working for an illusionist named Quandrasi?"

Vergil stared at Handri, momentarily dumfounded. "Actually," he murmured after a moment, "Grimble brought it up, but then denied it." As he would have done if he were trying to draw attention away from the idea. That would explain what Vergil had seen at the house: the illusionist had been pretending to be Grimble, and had for some reason decided to show his true form to Marko. But that was impossible. "He would be well over a hundred years old," Vergil said. If the illusionist were half-elven like Lord Brand he might still be alive, but he had certainly looked human to Vergil.

"So are you," Handri pointed out.

"Yes," Vergil replied impatiently, "but my preservation was due to the…" He trailed off, and from the look on Handri's face he was certain he was thinking the same thing. "Zelaznium," he finished. "You're thinking that Quandrasi discovered the preservative properties of zelaznium as well. That may be why he had it stolen in the first place!"

Handri nodded. "But if the man you saw at the house really was Quandrasi, what is he planning? Why did he abduct Marko?"

"And why has no one seen him for over a hundred years?" Vergil asked, frowning. "Has he been secretly planning something this whole time?"

Handri shrugged, having evidently exhausted his supply of insight for the moment. "You said you were chased from Grimble's house by goblins. Do the goblins know who he really is?"

Vergil thought for a moment. "He sent the CAGE goblins away. The goblins who chased me were wearing black uniforms of a sort I had not seen before. I suspect Quandrasi has a small coterie of goblins he keeps as a sort of elite personal guard. The black-uniformed guards may be aware of his secret."

Handri nodded thoughtfully. The carriage had arrived in front of Marko's apartment.

"Okay," said Vergil. "Time to give an ogre some bad news."

Fifteen

Vergil walked in the door of Marko's apartment to see Yurgi lying flat on her back, a goblin leaning over her. At first he thought one of the CAGE goons had returned to finish her off, but the goblin turned as they walked in and Vergil recognized her: Lagorna.

"What are you doing here?" Vergil asked.

"I was trying to help Handri find you," Lagorna said, a note of irritation in her voice. "It was quite rude of you to leave him that way, you know. And then you left Yurgi alone as well, and with a dislocated kneecap. She's lucky I showed up." Vergil saw that Yurgi's knee was wrapped in a bandage that seemed to have been torn from the bottom of her toga.

"She asked me to go after Marko!" said Vergil.

"Did you find him?" Yurgi asked hopefully. She lifted her head from the couch cushion it had been resting on to look behind Vergil and Handri, as if Marko might still be coming up the stairs.

"I found him," said Vergil. "And barely escaped to tell of it." He leaned heavily against the doorframe.

"Come inside, sir," said Handri, taking Vergil's arm. Vergil leaned on him and they made their way to the couch. Vergil sank into it with a groan and Handri took a seat in a chair next to him.

"Tell us what happened," said Lagorna. "Is Lord Balphry in a dungeon?"

"Not exactly," said Vergil. He proceeded to tell them everything that had happened. When he got to the part about Grimble turning into an old man, he glanced at Handri, uncertain whether he could trust them with this information. He was beginning to doubt he had even seen it. At this point he was so bewildered that he could only rely on Handri's judgment on such matters. Handri gave him a slight nod, and Vergil reluctantly told the rest of the story.

"I knew it!" cried Lagorna, which prompted everyone in the room to turn and stare at her.

"You knew what?" asked Handri, puzzled.

"That something had changed about Grimble. He's different. The past few months he's done nothing but stir up trouble. My cousin was a good friend of his when we were children, and she said he walked right past her on the street, acting like he didn't ever recognize her."

"So you think it's true," said Vergil. "Grimble really is the illusionist, Quandrasi."

"I don't know about that part," said Lagorna, "but he definitely isn't Grimble. At some point Grimble was replaced."

"So where is the real Grimble?" asked Handri.

"I suspect he is buried in a shallow grave outside of town," said Vergil. "If Quandrasi really has taken his place, he would not want the real Grimble to be discovered."

"Why would this Quandrasi go to so much trouble, though?" asked Lagorna. "What does he want?"

As if to answer her question, a piercing scream came through the window, followed by the shouts of men and goblins.

"Chaos," said Vergil. "Unrest. Discord. Grimble—that is, Quandrasi, if that is truly whom we are dealing with—is not merely attempting to suppress anti-goblin sentiment. He is deliberately overplaying his hand with CAGE to increase the strife between men and monsters."

"But why?" asked Handri. "What is the point?"

Vergil shook his head. "That I cannot say. I think Marko knows, though. Grimble—that is, Quandrasi—was clearly trying to persuade him of something. I suspect he was trying to enlist Marko in the cause. To Marko's credit, he seemed to refuse the offer."

"You said Quandrasi revealed himself shortly thereafter," said Lagorna. "Why do you think he did that?"

"It is difficult to say," said Vergil. "Perhaps he thought he could bring Marko over to his side by demonstrating his power. Or perhaps he merely wanted Marko to know who had beaten him."

"And Marko is still being held at Grimble's mansion?" asked Lagorna.

"As far as I know," said Vergil. "But as I said, I was observed at the scene. I suspect Marko will either be moved or placed under heavy guard."

"We have to rescue him," said Yurgi, pulling herself into a seated position. "I'm feeling much better now. My knee is still sore, but I can at least bend it now. And I won't let those stupid goblins sneak up on me this time." She blushed at looked at Lagorna. "Sorry, I didn't mean—"

"It's alright, Yurgi," said Lagorna. "They *are* stupid goblins. Not all goblins are stupid, but these are. Anyone with a bit of sense would have known there was something off with Grimble."

"But what will we do then?" asked Yurgi. "We can't let them throw Marko in a dungeon somewhere. He's delicate. He won't survive!"

Vergil nodded, thinking that Marko would be lucky if that were the worst Quandrasi did to him. If the illusionist really had been working on his scheme for a hundred years, murdering a single nobleman would seem like a small obstacle. "The only option that occurs to me," Vergil said, "would be to seek out allies amongst the other council members. When I overheard Thameril speaking with Grimble's agent, Bander, Thameril seemed dubious of the wisdom of Grimble's plan. That is, of Quandrasi's plan. I apologize; I am having difficulty adjusting my understanding of the situation to account for the latest empirical data. Such has been my lot since awaking from my accursed slumber."

"You think we could convince Thameril to stand up to Quandrasi?" asked Lagorna.

"It sounded to me as if Quandrasi was using evidence of Thameril's involvement in KLAMP as leverage against him. Bander threatened to reveal Thameril's connections with that gang of hooligans if he refused to go along with his plan to abduct me. That is, what I thought at the time was his plan to abduct me, but what turns out to have been a plan to abduct Marko. But Thameril seems like a generally reasonable man to me; if we can convince him that he has more to lose by allowing Quandrasi's schemes to go forward, I think he will join us in resisting him."

"But we don't know what Quandrasi's scheme is," said Handri.

"No, but we know that he seems to be fomenting chaos in Avaressa, and that can't be good for a man like Thameril, who relies on a compliant populace to keep his position."

"And if we do convince Thameril that Quandrasi is dangerous, then what?" asked Handri. "What is our plan?"

"One thing at a time, good Handri," said Vergil. "Perhaps Thameril can help us formulate a plan. That is one more reason to seek him out."

Handri shook his head. "I don't like it," he said. "Relying on politicians is never a good idea."

"This is the hand we were dealt, I'm afraid," replied Vergil. "We can seek out Thameril or we can cower in fear. Unless you have other connections with highly-placed individuals, I do not see any other options."

"We can flee," said Handri. "Fleeing is an option."

"I had assumed fleeing was included under the broader category of cowering in fear," said Vergil.

"But they're two different things!" Handri protested.

"Fair enough," replied Vergil. "We have three options, two of which are motivated by cowardice."

"That's better," said Handri.

"I maintain, however, that submitting to cowardice is not a desirable option."

"Then you will go to see Thameril in the morning?" asked Lagorna.

"Given the urgency of the situation, I would suggest we seek him out now," Vergil said. "Assuming we can find him. He is unlikely to be in the council building at this hour."

"He lives in the mayor's residence," said Lagorna. "Just down the street from the council building. Big green house with fluted columns out front. You can't miss it."

Vergil nodded. He had walked past the house before nearly running into Thameril the previous day. In the distance, a bell chimed. It chimed twice more and then, after a short pause, chimed three more times.

"What is that?" asked Vergil.

"Curfew in one hour," said Lagorna. "No one allowed on the streets after sunset."

"Curfew?" asked Handri. "Is there usually a curfew?"

"Only in extreme emergencies," said Lagorna. "There hasn't been one since the Zaltani barbarians last attacked twenty years ago. Things must be really getting out of hand if the council is instituting one now."

"Well, it's too dangerous to go out in the daytime," said Handri. "We'll be seen. Grimble—I mean, Quandrasi—must have half of the CAGE goons out looking for you. Probably the city guard too."

"Then we wait until dark," said Vergil.

"But the curfew," Handri said. "We'll be the only ones on the street. They'll catch us for sure."

"We have no choice," said Vergil. "I doubt we'd make it to Thameril's house and back before dark anyway. And I need to eat something before I pass out."

"Right," said Lagorna, getting to her feet. "I will get us some food and bring it back here."

"Are we safe here?" asked Handri. "I'm surprised Quandrasi hasn't sent any of his goons here to look for Vergil yet. Seems like the first place he would look."

Vergil frowned and rubbed his chin. He had been so distracted by everything going on that it hadn't occurred to him how dangerous it was to be in Marko's apartment.

"I can handle those goons," said Yurgi.

"Are you certain, Yurgi?" said Vergil. "Your last encounter with them argues to the contrary."

"I told you, they took me by surprise," Yurgi said, a bit offended. "I was sleeping when they broke in, and they got me in the knee with a lucky shot. I'm not going to let that happen again." She slowly stood up, clearly favoring her right leg. She winced as she put weight on the bad knee, and Vergil frowned at her. "It hurts a little," she said, "but I'll be okay. Even with a bad knee, I can take twenty goblins in a fair fight."

"Speaking as a goblin," said Lagorna, "I can tell you goblins will never choose a fair fight when there's another option. But as I'm unlikely to be of much help either way, I'll go find some food. If you're all dead when I get back, I'm keeping it all for myself." When they stared at her in horror, she added, "That was a joke." Still not getting any response, she shrugged and walked out the door.

While Yurgi slowly paced the floor, trying to loosen up her knee, Vergil leaned back on the couch, resting his sore joints and weary muscles. Handri sat next to him, staring blankly into space, his apelike arms hanging at his side and his belly protruding under his shirt. Vergil couldn't help laughing at the sight of them. If this group was Avaress' only hope for restoring order and sanity, Dis had fallen on hard times indeed.

Vergil might have fallen asleep if it weren't for the near-constant noise outside: dogs barking, horses whinnying, agitated voices, sometimes the sound of glass breaking or the occasional scream. It hadn't yet reached the level of cacophony, but the situation in the city was definitely deteriorating.

Lagorna returned about half an hour later, looking frazzled and frightened, with several paper packages. "I don't envy you having to go out into that after dark," she said. "Maybe things will calm down after the curfew, but I suspect the worst element of the city is still in hiding, waiting for the dark. The whole city feels like it is on edge."

She unwrapped the packages, which turned out to contain bread, meat, and cheese, and placed the food on the small table in front of them. Lagorna, Vergil and Handri dug in, but Yurgi held back, continuing to work her injured knee.

"You have to eat, Yurgi," said Lagorna. "There isn't much, but you should have something."

Yurgi shook her head. "That's not even a snack for me. Better not to have anything. It's okay, sometimes ogres go days without eating."

Vergil supposed this was true. Of course, humans sometimes went days without eating as well, but that didn't mean it was easy for them. He suspected that Yurgi was punishing herself for her failure to keep Marko safe. Before today it had never even occurred to him that ogres could experience such emotions—let alone for a member of an entirely different species. Was Yurgi a particularly sensitive ogre, or had Vergil been wrong about them as well?

As the three of them finished off the food, the bell chimed three times again, indicating that the curfew had begun. The sun had set, and the sky outside the southern window was reddish-gray.

Vergil forced himself to get up from the couch, doing his best to ignore his stiff joints. "It is time, Handri," he said, trying to sound enthusiastic. "I would go alone, but I am not entirely certain my bones will get me there. I may need to lean on you."

"You're always welcome to lean on me, sir," said Handri, "if you're certain this is the correct course of action."

"I have not been certain of anything since I woke up three weeks ago," said Vergil. "And I have begun to retroactively doubt many things I had been certain of before that. But I don't see that we have much choice at present. We have to go talk to Thameril."

"Then I will go with you," said Handri.

"I will stay with Yurgi," said Lagorna. "If you're not back by morning, we will—"

"We'll be back," said Handri. "You helped us, and we're not going to abandon you. Right, Vergil?"

"Right," said Vergil, after a moment's hesitation. He wasn't entirely certain he wanted to cast his lot with an ogre and a goblin, despite his rapidly evolving sentiments on monsters. But he supposed that if he and Handri survived their errand and weren't captured, they would have to come back. Where else would they go?

Vergil and Handri made their way down the stairs, Vergil continuing to lean heavily on Handri's shoulder. Vergil wasn't sure how they were going to make it across town to Thameril's house in this condition—particularly since there weren't any cabs available. They had no choice but to walk the whole way.

Handri peered around the corner of the doorway and, apparently having concluded the street was clear, tugged on Vergil's arm. The two of them proceeded across the street and down a dark alley, Vergil using Handri for occasional support. He found that as he walked, he began to feel a bit better. The rest earlier in the day had done him good; the bed of weeds by the side of the road had actually been more comfortable than the mattress he had slept on in Goblintown. The food had energized him, and walking was helping to loosen up his joints some. The sky was cloudy, the veiled moon giving them just enough light to see where they were going. Vergil began to think they might actually make it to Thameril's house without incident. They could hear shouts and other sounds of mayhem in the distance, and orange glows on the horizon indicated that several fires were burning somewhere to the north and east, but the streets here seemed relatively quiet.

Then, as they approached a street, Vergil heard footsteps approaching rapidly from the left. They hung back, pressing themselves against a wall so as not to be seen. Moments later a slight, wiry figure—clearly a goblin—sprinted past. Somewhere to the left a man shouted something incomprehensible, and the sound of several more men running followed. They watched as a group of men, armed with clubs and other makeshift weapons, ran past the alley after the goblin. The man in the lead carried a torch.

"Looks like the coast is clear," said Handri, looking down the street after them. "If we cross here, I think we can take mostly side streets the rest of the way.

"Hmm," said Vergil, watching the men disappear down the street.

"Sir Vergil, it's none of our business," said Handri. "We're on a mission. We can't allow ourselves to be sidetracked."

Vergil nodded. There was some truth to what Handri said. They had no idea why these men were chasing the goblin; perhaps he was a thief or arsonist. In any case, the fate of one goblin wouldn't matter if they failed to get the city under control. Many more—both goblins and human—would be imprisoned or killed if the chaos continued to escalate. And yet, ironically, the same chivalric principles that once prompted him to champion humanity against goblins were now goading him to assist the lone goblin.

"It is unsportsmanlike," he said. "That many men against one goblin."

"I thought you'd be happy it was humans chasing a goblin, rather than the other way around."

"All things considered, yes," said Vergil. "But still…"

Handri sighed. "Alright, if we're going to do this, let's do it."

"Right!" said Vergil. "After me." He darted down the street after the men just in time to see the last one disappear around a corner. He and Handri approached the corner, finding themselves looking down an alley lit only by the torch held by the man at the head of the group. Behind him—closer to Vergil and Handri—were several more men; Vergil counted eight in total. Craning his neck to look past them, Vergil saw the goblin cringing in the corner. He was younger than Vergil had at first thought, just a kid really. It wasn't entirely clear what the men were going to do to him, but it was a safe bet they weren't promoting an after-school tutoring program.

"Hello, there!" exclaimed Vergil, as the men moved to surround the young goblin. Taken by surprise, the men turned to regard the newcomers. "I am Vergil, Knight of the Order of the Unyielding Badger, and this is my faithful squire Handri. This city is currently under curfew. We demand to know by what authority you remain on the street, and what you intend to do with the frightened young chap who has just wet himself in fright." It was true; the evidence was currently making its way down the poor goblin's trousers.

Appealing to the men's respect for authority was a bold gambit, and it might have worked if the man with the torch hadn't recognized them. "Hey," he said, "aren't you that knight that was supposed to help us chase off those goblin refugees the other night?" Nods and murmurs of assent indicated that this wasn't the only man who had been present during Vergil's unfortunate tryout with KLAMP.

"Well, yes," said Vergil. "But I don't see what that has to do with—"

"Go back to sleep, old man," another jeered. "You're out of your element." The three closest men were now approaching Vergil, brandishing their clubs.

"Sir," said Handri, has hand on Vergil's shoulder, "perhaps we should go. You are in no shape to fight. If you are volunteering to be bludgeoned, I will not desert you, but I do not see how our presence helps this young goblin any."

"I knew it," sneered the man closest to Vergil. He was tall, with shaggy brown hair. He clutched a length of steel pipe in his hands. "You two are goblin-lovers. I could tell the moment you showed up the other night. You don't realize the threat these monsters pose to humanity."

At this, Vergil stiffened, his fear giving way to anger. "You, sir," he said, wagging his finger at the man, "are a fool."

A puzzled expression came over the tall man's face. "Pardon me?" he asked.

"No, I think not," said Vergil, taking a step forward. "You have not the faintest idea what an actual threat is. You live in prosperous city, filled with wonders and opportunity, free of the specter of attack by brigands or barbarians. You've never seen a village burned to the ground or a family hiding for days in a cellar. You use the language of war and invasion, yet you fear not armies but caravans of desperate families looking for work and a place to lay their heads. Some knights you are, ganging up on one young, unarmed goblin and cornering him in an alley. What is your intention now, o valiant heroes? Do you plan to take turns holding this whelp down while you pummel him with your clubs? Will that spare your precious city from the great evil you fear?"

"I fear nothing!" growled the tall man. "I wish only to rid my city of this monstrous scum."

Vergil nodded. "I will take you at your word," he said. He pointed to a squat, mustached man standing next to him, holding a long wooden cudgel. "You, give your weapon to the goblin."

The first man snorted. "You've lost your mind, old man."

"You claim to be afraid of nothing," said Vergil. "And yet it would appear that you are afraid of a stripling of a goblin armed with a cudgel. You are not only a fool, but a liar and a coward as well."

The men stood around uncertainly for a moment. They clearly wanted to get back to their business with the goblin, but they seemed to be unsure how to deal with Vergil. Finally one of them spoke up, "Just give him the cudgel, Marlin. Salaman can handle one goblin."

Several of the men clearly had misgivings about this idea, but none of them wanted to go on record as thinking that Salaman was a coward. After some mumbling and feet-shuffling, Marlin broke the impasse by stepping forward and handing the cudgel to the goblin, who accepted it as if he were being handed a dead cat. The goblin stood blinking uncertainly, tears glistening on his cheeks. It was fairly clear he had never held a weapon in his life. Salaman scowled at Vergil, but turned and walked toward the goblin. The man with the torch stood just to his right, illuminating the two would-be combatants. The others backed off, forming a semi-circle around them in the narrow alley. Vergil and Handri stood in the back, seemingly forgotten.

"Is this a good idea?" Handri whispered. "That goblin could still get beat up pretty bad."

"At least he has a fighting chance now," said Vergil. "Although I suspect he will not need to put up much of a fight. Watch."

As they watched, Salaman took a step toward the goblin, taking an awkward swing with his pipe, which the goblin easily blocked with the cudgel. The goblin swung half-heartedly at him, and Salaman held up the pipe to block. He misjudged the point of impact, though, and the cudgel bounced off his knuckles.

"Gaaahhh!" Salaman cried, dropping the pipe, which fell on his foot. Salaman howled in pain and fell to the ground, gripping his foot. The goblin was so startled that he not only dropped his cudgel, but somehow managed to wet himself even more. Each aspiring gladiator was for some time too preoccupied with his own situation even to take notice of his foe.

"This is the worst fight I've ever seen," said Handri.

"That is because you did not witness me facing off against the goblins who abducted Zelaznus." Vergil replied.

"Was that worse?"

Vergil watched as Salaman lay on the ground, clutching his foot and moaning. A few feet away the goblin began to sob as urine saturated his shoes. The rest of the men continued to stand around, unsure of how to proceed.

"I lack the proper perspective to judge fairly," said Vergil. He raised his voice to speak to the group. "All right, gentlemen, I believe you have made your point. This goblin has been sufficiently terrified for the evening. There is little doubt you all will be figuring prominently in his nightmares for the next several weeks, so you can consider this a job well done."

The men grumbled and looked at each other, but the fight had gone out of them. They had wanted to engage in a mob beating of an anonymous goblin, not face off with a frightened kid. The men filed past Vergil, some of them dropping their weapons as they passed. Salamin, hopping on his good foot, brought up the rear. He avoided looking Vergil in the eye.

The goblin had stopped sobbing, but now he was regarding Vergil and Handri fearfully, as if perhaps they had chased the men off only to pummel him themselves.

"Have no fear, young goblin," said Vergil. "We mean you no harm. These streets are dangerous, though, and you are in violation of the curfew. I would suggest you hightail it home."

The goblin nodded. "Th-thanks," he said. "I will." He shuffled past them toward the street.

"By the way," said Vergil, "why were they chasing you?"

"Oh," said the goblin, stopping to face them, a sheepish grin creeping across his face. "I burned down a store."

Sixteen

Unprepared to mete out justice to the young goblin—and having a bit of a soft spot for arsonists—Vergil let him go with a warning, and Vergil and Handri continued on their way to Thameril's house. They had to backtrack several blocks to avoid a band of looters wreaking havoc on one of the main commercial streets, and then nearly ran right into a contingent of the city guard on its way to deal with the looting. Presumably the CAGE goons were out in force as well, but fortunately Vergil and Handri didn't encounter any of them. At one point Vergil rounded a corner to see a great looming figure bearing down on him, but he realized after a moment of sheer panic that it was *Unity*—the unfinished statue in the center of the city square. The damned thing was actually some distance away, but it was so gigantic that he had at first taken it for an ogre.

"What is it, sir?" asked Handri, coming up behind him. "Oh."

"Just startled me a bit," said Vergil. "That thing is like something out of a—" But his train of thought was broken by a crash of breaking glass from a building across the square.

"Let's go, sir. It isn't safe to be out in the open."

"All right," said Vergil.

They skirted the edge of the square then cut through an alley toward a residential neighborhood. It took nearly two hours to get to the mayor's residence altogether, but Vergil felt surprisingly well despite the day's ordeals. He was tired and his joints still hurt, but he found that he could walk without Handri's assistance. Fortunately, they hadn't needed to do any more running since their encounter with the men chasing the goblin, skulking and hiding being sufficient to keep them out of trouble. This part of town in particular was surprisingly quiet. Two city guardsmen stood outside the entrance of the big house, looking sleepy and bored. Lanterns burned on posts lining the street here, providing just enough illumination for them to make out the faces of the guards—which probably explained why hooligans were avoiding the area.

Vergil and Handri watched the guards from the shadows for some time, debating whether to try to sneak around the back of the house or approach the guards directly. For once, Handri argued for the direct approach, while Vergil thought it wiser to try to remain unseen. They were unarmed and in no condition for a fight; if the guards turned them away, they'd have blown their chance to secure their one possible ally in the city. And that was assuming the guards hadn't been ordered to arrest them on sight.

But Vergil had had enough sneaking around and peering in windows—and sprinting and wall-climbing were out of the question. "I am going to approach the guards and plead our case," said Vergil. "I will consider it no slight if you would prefer to remain in the shadows, good Handri. You have already proven your loyalty more than I could reasonably have expected."

But Handri shook his head. "If you intend to speak to the guards, I will come with you."

"Very good," said Vergil. "Then let us skulk no longer." He straightened his jacket and stepped out of the shadows. He strode down the center of the road toward the guards, Handri following close behind. When they were only a few paces away, one of the not terribly observant guards stiffened and called out, "Who goes there?"

"It is I, Sir Vergil Parmeligo, knight of the Order of the Unyielding Badger, and my faithful squire Handri." Handri was not, of course, technically his squire, but the suggestion that Vergil had a squire added something to his prestige, and Handri didn't seem to mind. "We request an audience with Mayor Thameril."

The guards looked at each other. One of them shrugged. "Okay," he said. "Wait here." He turned and walked up the steps to the house, opened the door, and disappeared inside.

"Nice night," offered Handri, as the other guard continued to stand staring off into space. "Other than the rioting, arson and looting, I mean."

The guard shrugged almost imperceptibly.

A few moments later the other guard reemerged from the house. "Go on in," he said. "Thameril is in the sitting room." He returned to his post as Vergil and Handri nodded in thanks, walking past him up the steps.

"That was easier than I expected," said Handri.

"Be thankful for small favors," said Vergil. "A warrant for our arrest has apparently not been issued to the city guard."

They went inside, finding Thameril sitting on the floor in the midst of a boxes half-filled with books, clothing, and other sundries. In front of him was a pile of silverware; he was muttering and buffing a tarnished serving spoon with the front of his shirt.

"Good heavens," Vergil said. "What is all this, Thameril?"

"Eh?" Thameril said, looking up. "Oh, Sir Virgil. And, um…"

"Handri."

"Right," said Thameril. "I'm fleeing. This city is done for."

"You can't flee!" cried Handri. "We were counting on you to help us restore order!"

"Restore order?" said Thameril with a frown. "No, we're well past that. Whatever progress has been made in goblin-human relations over the past century has been undone. The lines of civil war are being drawn, and whatever the outcome of that conflict, this whole city is going to burn. You would be wise to flee as well. CAGE has rounded up all the small fish they can find; they've moved on to noblemen. Doesn't matter if they're involved in KLAMP or not. Grimble is just looking for scapegoats. If I didn't know better, I'd say he's *trying* to stir up discord in the city. And doing a damn fine job."

"That is what we came to tell you," Vergil said. "That is exactly what Grimble is doing. Except that he is not Grimble."

"What do you mean, he's not Grimble?" said Thameril, looking up from his spoon.

There was no point in mincing words now, Vergil realized. If they were going to have any chance of recruiting Thameril to their side, they had to impress upon him the seriousness of the situation.

"We believe the goblin you know as Grimble is in fact the illusionist Quandrasi. At some point Quandrasi replaced the real Grimble, most likely killing him in the process, and has been posing as him in order to sow the seeds of discord in the city."

Thameril stared at Vergil for a moment, then burst out laughing. "Quandrasi? The mythical illusionist who was supposedly behind the zelaznium theft a century ago? If he ever existed—and most historians believe he did not—he would be a hundred and fifty years old! Stop looking for grand quests where there is only pettiness and incompetence. I'll admit Grimble has getting a bit more ornery of late, but Grimble is just Grimble."

"That is where you are wrong," said a voice from behind them. "Grimble has not been Grimble for some time now." Turning to face the newcomer, Vergil was surprised to see Bander, Grimble's messenger, stride into the room, holding the the staff with the silver globe. Two black-uniformed goblins armed with swords came in after and moved to flank him. Two more of the elite guard followed them.

"Bander?" asked Thameril. "What in Grovlik's name are you doing here?"

"Haven't you been listening?" said Bander. "Old Vergil here is a delusional old fool, but he was right about me. Quandrasi the illusionist at your service. You have known me for the past six months as the Grimble the goblin."

"You don't look anything like Grimble," said Thameril.

"That's why it's called an illusion, genius," Bander replied. "I could prove it to you right now if I wanted to, but it changing my form requires a bit of effort and I frankly don't care if you believe me or not. You'll believe soon enough. Seize them!"

This command was directed to the black-uniformed goblins, who moved past Bander into the room. One of them grabbed Vergil, twisting his arms behind his back and expertly wrapping his wrists with twine. Handri seemed on the verge of resisting, but seeing that Vergil did not, he silently put his hands behind his back and let another goblin do the same to him. Thameril did not go so quietly. Two of the goblins hauled him to his feet while he howled that he was the mayor, they would never get away with this, etc., until he found himself standing with this wrists tied next to Vergil and it seemed to dawn on him that neither the city guard nor anyone else was going to come to his aid. Vergil stood agape. Had Bander been Quandrasi all along as well?

"I have to admit," Bander said, as he regarded his three captives, "I am impressed you were able to determine my true identity. I thought I had laid low long enough that no one would make the connection. But of course I hadn't counted on the meddling of someone who had laid low almost as long as I had."

"So it really is you," said Vergil. "You were Bander and Grimble. Anyone else we should know about?"

Bander-Quandrasi shrugged. "I occasionally take other forms when trying to remain unnoticed, but no one important. At least not for some time. You'd never have known if it weren't for your tresspassing."

"It was Handri that figured it out," said Vergil. "For what it's worth."

"Indeed?" said Bander-Quandrasi, looking at Handri. "It seems I have underestimated your sidekick. But it is still you, Vergil, to whom I owe the greatest debt."

"What are you talking about?" asked Vergil, scowling. "What debt?"

"To answer that," Bander-Quandrasi replied "I have to go back a bit. You see, I have been waiting a very long time for the perfect moment to execute my plan. It is because of you that moment has finally come—and that I am still here to execute it. Well over a century ago I built my lair in the Adelia Mountains, on the border between the human lands and the lands of monsters. Over the next several years I used my skills as an illusionist to sow distrust between the various races of Dis. I employed all manner of tricks to promote this goal. I might, for example, incite a band of hooligans to raid a neighboring town and use a spell to disguise the attackers as goblins, or make a goblin chief's rival appear to be the chief's brother so that the rival could get close enough to assassinate the chief—and then, when the assassin flees, change his appearance to that of a human. In this way I contributed to the gradual deterioration of relations between humans and monsters.

"Why would you do that?" asked Vergil, baffled. "What is the end game of all of this intrigue and provocation?"

"I'm doing a sort of dramatic reveal here," said Bander-Quandrasi, scowling at the interruption. "For now, suffice it to say that my plans require a certain level of interspecies discord. If I may be allowed to continue: when Lord Brand began to form his monstrous army, I was at first elated, thinking that an all-out war was exactly what I needed to complete my plan. But as the monsters were drawn to Brandsveid, the tension on the border actually lessened, as there was less intermingling between the races. When war finally came, it was over in a matter of days—and then, infuriatingly, rather than press his advantage, Brand withdrew his troops within Brandsveid and set about the process of making peace with the other kingdoms. It became clear to me that I had missed my chance and that I would probably have to wait a long time for another opportunity to present itself. Fortunately, Vergil, you provided me with a solution. You see, I had masterminded the theft of zelaznium for a very specific purpose, but you demonstrated a property of this wondrous element of which I had previously been unaware."

"Preservation," said Vergil. "Longevity."

"Yes," replied Bander-Quandrasi. "I had many spies throughout Avaress and the other kingdoms, and I began to hear stories about a knight who had been asleep for many years after inhaling a cloud of zelaznium powder. It was said, in fact, that this man did not seem to age. You had only been asleep for about twenty years at this point, so it was not yet evident that you *were* still aging, albeit at a slower rate than normal. Inhaling zelaznium is a rather uncommon pastime, and of course it occurred to me that this knight was the very same man who had interfered in my attempt to acquire the zelaznium from the Zelaznus himself. Oh! I nearly forgot to mention: this is not our first meeting. I was there that night, when you caught up with those goblins. I suppose a demonstration is in order. Very well."

He closed his eyes, and his body was momentarily engulfed in a strange shimmering—the same effect Vergil had seen through the window of Grimble's house. When the shimmer faded, an oddly familiar goblin, wearing tribal skins and a steel helmet, stood before him. "I am Khotem, chief of the Cholanthi tribe," said the figure solemnly, then broke into a giggle.

"It was you!" Vergil cried. "You didn't just bribe those goblins to steal the zelaznium, you took part in the theft yourself!"

"Correct," said the Khotem figure. He began to shimmer again, and a few seconds later he was replaced by the figure of Grimble. He grinned at Thameril, who paled visibly. After another moment, the shimmering engulfed Grimble, then faded to leave the old man in the blue robe, Quandrasi in his natural form—at least as far as Vergil knew. The strain of changing his form was evident in his face; sweat beaded on his brow and he pressed his hand against the wall to steady himself. After a moment, he continued, "I generally prefer to orchestrate my schemes from afar, but after initially agreeing to my offer, Chief Khotem attempted to renegotiate the terms. I found it necessary to remove him and temporarily take his place in the clan. My mistake was getting greedy: when we came upon Zelaznus working in his laboratory, I couldn't resist abducting the old alchemist in an attempt to learn some of his secrets. That prompted you to pursue us, which ultimately resulted in you foiling the theft. Of course, I assumed that no one could survive inhaling that amount of zelaznium; it wasn't until years later, when I heard about the mysterious comatose knight, that it occurred to me you were still alive.

"Not content to rely on gossip, I went to visit you at your estate outside Avaressa. Oh yes, Vergil. Made myself invisible and slipped right past your caretaker—a far more respectable-looking man than this ape, I might add. I stood at your bedside and watched you sleep for some time. I thought about smothering you in revenge for your meddling, but decided it wasn't worth the trouble. And it's a good thing I didn't: I had no idea at that point that you would someday awaken and that additional meddling on your part would greatly accelerate my plans. I had expected to spend several years as Grimble, gradually escalating tensions between humans and goblins, but your razing of the Goblintex mill was a masterstroke. Everything you've done since you've awoken has made my job easier.

"But I'm getting ahead of myself. My intent the day I came to your home was only to determine whether my suspicions about the preservative properties of zelaznium were correct, and I could see that they were: you appeared to have aged not a day since I had last seen you, nearly twenty years earlier. Since that time I had managed—at great personal expense—to get my hands on a small supply of zelaznium to replace the quantity you had taken from me, and I decided to experiment with it in small quantities to see if I could replicate the effect. I returned to my lair, inhaled a tiny pinch of the stuff, and immediately fell into a deep sleep lasting three months. When I awoke, I conferred with my spies regarding the current political and social climate in the region, concluding that circumstances were not yet amenable to my plan. I went back to sleep for another three months.

"This is how I spent most of the next seventy years, patiently waiting for relations between humans and monsters to deteriorate, and occasionally hiring new servants and seeking out spies to replace those who had died. I was at first hopeful when the leaders of the Six Kingdoms worked out deals with Brandsveid to allow monsters to immigrate to their lands, thinking that this unnatural commingling of races would bring about the discord I desired. Sadly, it turns out that humans and monsters can coexist perfectly well; racial antipathy seems to be primarily an artifact of economic inequality and poverty. It wasn't until the economic boom caused by Brand's innovations finally ended that economic conditions deteriorated to the point where animosity and humans and monsters began to reemerge. That was when I decided it was time to recommence my plan. After laying some groundwork, I took the place of Grimble on the city council, and here we are."

"You mean you murdered Grimble," said Thameril.

Quandrasi shrugged, as if this were a semantic point.

"You still haven't told us what this is all about," said Vergil. "What is the point of stirring up all this animosity and hatred?"

"Sorry," said Quandrasi. "Got a little sidetracked with the background information there. Rest assured all your hard work has not been for naught, Vergil. I must ask that you indulge me a bit longer, though, if you are going to understand what it is I am trying to accomplish. I am, as you know, an illusionist. I work in the realm of perception and emotion. People like to believe that this realm is somehow separate from the everyday reality which we occupy. But nothing could be further from the truth. Our reality *is* perception and emotion. Other than what our senses tell us and how we feel about those sensations, there is no reality. And I don't mean merely that our minds create the world that each of us individually occupies—although that's as far as most illusionists ever pursue the matter. I learned early on in my studies that the minds of a large number of sentient beings, when appropriately manipulated into certain shared thought patterns, can actually reach out to manipulate physical reality."

"I fail to comprehend your baroque language," said Vergil. "Are you speaking of some sort of shared delusion?"

"I am indeed," said Quandrasi, "but that is merely the beginning. You see, I learned that the most powerful human emotion—and the easiest to manipulate—is fear. Closely related to fear is hatred, and it is the power of hatred that I intend to harness. All I need to do is provoke a large portion of the citizens of this city to a fierce, unreasoning hatred. It matters not to whom or what this fear is directed. Already the populace is near the boiling point, and at noon tomorrow, with the execution of Lord Balphry—"

"You're going to execute Marko?" Vergil gasped.

"Well, not I personally," said Quandrasi. "But yes, that's the idea. After whipping the crowd into hate-fueled frenzy, of course. I plan to have a sort of show trial, featuring Marko and several members of the city council, including the mayor here. Nothing personal, Thameril; I just need someone the crowd can blame for the result troubles in the city. Everyone in the city is angry; they just need someone to direct their anger toward. Since you're here, Vergil, I may as well include you as well."

"Why?" asked Vergil again. "Just tell us what you are trying to accomplish, blast you!"

"If you stop interrupting," Quandrasi snapped, "I'll tell you. You're really draining the impact from the villain monologue I'm doing here. You see, the idea is to channel the crowd's hatred into physical form, bringing into being a—"

At that moment the door swung open, and through the doorway Vergil could see the lower two thirds of a very large, toga-clad individual: Yurgi. She ducked doorway and hobbled inside, clearly favoring her right leg.

The goblins gaped dumbly at Yurgi; if they noticed her handicap, they didn't seem particularly encouraged by it. It was one thing for a dozen goblins to take an ogre by surprise; it was quite another for four of them to face her in a fair fight. Quandrasi seemed more irritated than afraid, as if he were upset that this latest development was going to require some recalibration of his plan.

"Let them go!" Yurgi roared, taking another step into the room.

"Back off or I'll kill him!" yelled one of the goblins near Thameril, drawing his sword to emphasize the point.

Yurgi cocked her head at Thameril, but there was no hint of recognition in her eyes. She shrugged and proceeded to stomp awkwardly across the room toward the goblin, who was so terrified at the sight of the massive creature bearing down on him that he completely forgot about his threat, dropped his sword, and ran out of the room. The other goblins, realizing that threatening to eviscerate their captives wasn't going to save them, followed his example.

Yurgi pursued the goblins out of the room, oblivious to Quandrasi, who had stepped out of the way to let her by. Vergil thought at first that perhaps the illusionist had used some kind of spell to make himself invisible to her, but concluded that Yurgi simply didn't consider the old man to be a threat. She had identified the goblins as the instigators, and was determined to pursue them. Quandrasi regarded the others still in the room, sighed, and then muttered something under his breath.

"Get him!" Vergil cried, but it was already too late. A cloud of thick black smoke was billowing forth from the floor around the illusionist, and soon had enveloped him completely. Virgil ran forward, his hands still tied behind his back, attempting to intercept Quandrasi as he ran, but encountered nothing until his forehead smacked against the far wall. He staggered back, now completely blinded by the smoke. This smoke wasn't noxious like that which had filled the mill when it was burning; in fact, it seemed to have no real substance at all. It served only to blot out all the light in the room.

"Sir, where are you?" said Handri's voice, a few feet away.

"I am over here, Handri. I'm afraid our malevolent prestidigitator has escaped."

Vergil felt Handri's shoulder brush against his arm. Handri's hand clutched his sleeve. "This way, sir. I think."

The two of them stumbled in the dark for some time, their hands tied behind their backs, with Handri doing his best to guide Vergil in the direction of the door. Eventually he found the front wall and shuffled along it until they got to the the doorway. They made their way outside. A few paces away from the house, the smoke dissipated. Lagorna the goblin stood in the street waiting for them. Other than Lagorna, the street was empty. Bander-Quandrasi must have dismissed the city guard.

"Yurgi was worried about you," Lagorna said. "I told her you'd be fine, but she was sure you had run into trouble. Evidently she was right."

"We had the misfortune of showing up just before Quandrasi came to arrest Thameril," said Vergil. "It is only because of Yurgi that we escaped. I couldn't tell you where she's gone, though. And Quandrasi seems to have slipped away as well."

"So it really was him?" Lagorna said. "An old man with a staff ran past me a moment ago. I would have come in, but Yurgi made me promise to stay outside. Said I would only be in the way. She was probably right."

As she spoke, Thameril staggered out of the house.

"Is Quandrasi gone?" Thameril asked urgently.

"So it would appear," said Vergil, "although one should be skeptical of appearances when an illusionist is at large."

"Wasn't that Marko's ogress, Yurgi? Is she a friend of yours?"

"More or less," said Vergil.

Thameril nodded, looking back at the house. "How long do you think it will take for that smoke to clear? Or whatever it is. I need to finish packing."

"You cannot be serious," said Vergil. "Do you not see the danger this city faces? We need your help!"

"There is nothing I can do about it," said Thameril. "I'm more determined than ever to get out of town. If Quandrasi's goons get his hands on me again, I'm finished. It was luck that ogress showed up, but I'm not counting on that kind of intervention happening again. Seriously, is this stuff ever going to clear? Should I get a fan?"

"I'm afraid he's right," said Lagorna. "Quandrasi apparently now has the city guard on his side. Between them and the CAGE goons, we don't have a chance. The KLAMP leadership has all been imprisoned, and Marko's attempts to encourage a more mainstream resistance have failed. This city is doomed."

"What are you saying?" asked Handri. "You're not going to help us either?"

"What can I do?" asked Lagorna. "I already risked my neck to save you two. My husband is dead and I have two children. What's going to happen to them if Quandrasi decides I'm another obstacle to his plan? No, I'm done chasing you two all over town. I'm taking my family somewhere safe. Goodnight, all." With that she turned and walked away down the street.

"She's pretty smart for a goblin," said Thameril. "You would be wise to leave town as well, Vergil. You are an old man now, and in no shape to resist this illusionist. He's had us all fooled for months, maneuvering us like chess pieces to bring about his grand plan. It's foolishness to think we can fight him now. He's only revealed himself because he knows he can't be stopped."

"But we've got to try," said Handri. "I never liked Lord Balphry much, but he doesn't deserve to be executed. Not like this, for sure."

"Marko is a scheming, greedy, egotistical blowhard," said Thameril.

"Such traits did not constitute a capital offense in my time," said Vergil.

"Well, they certainly don't justify me risking my neck."

"Do you not feel any sense of responsibility?" asked Vergil. "We are all to some degree responsible for the current sad state of affairs in this city. Certainly I have contributed my share to the discord, and Marko is undoubtedly not blameless, but I am well aware of your ties to KLAMP. Things never would have gotten this far if it weren't for those fool vigilantes terrifying innocent goblins."

"That's exactly what I'm saying," Thameril replied. "Grimble— I mean, Quandrasi—put me up to that. He was subtle about it—so subtle, in fact, that for a while I entertained the thought that KLAMP was my idea. But later on I realized that he'd been manipulating me all along. He wanted KLAMP to get out of control, so that he would have an excuse to let CAGE loose. Don't you see? He's been five moves ahead of everyone from the beginning. Whatever he's planning for tomorrow, I don't want to be anywhere near it. Goodnight, gentlemen." He turned and went back inside, waving his hands in front of him. He left the door open, and Vergil could hear him opening windows and cursing to himself.

"It looks like it is just you and I, Handri," said Vergil. "Although I cannot in good conscience ask you to stay either."

"You're stuck with me, sir. But what will we do?"

"I do not know," admitted Vergil. "But we have until noon tomorrow to figure out how to stop Marko's execution. Perhaps if we can somehow disrupt Quandrasi's farce trial, we can stop his evil plan. And then try to repair some of the damage that has been done to this fine city."

"But what is his evil plan?" asked Handri. "Yurgi interrupted him before he had a chance to tell us."

"He said something about channeling the crowd's hatred into physical form, but I cannot for the life of me make sense of that statement. Not in my present condition, anyway. I need sleep, Handri. I can barely stand."

"Where will we go?" asked Handri. "We aren't safe at Marko's apartment. The front door won't even close."

"It's the only option we have," said Vergil. "We will have to hope that Quandrasi doesn't think to go back there."

Handri nodded, and they made their way back across town to the apartment, Vergil shambling like a zombie down the dark streets after Handri. Fortunately, although they still saw fires burning in the distance and the occasional scream or crash of breaking glass, they didn't run into any more trouble. By the time they arrived at Marko's building, Vergil was beyond exhausted. If any of the CAGE goons showed up, they were done for. They could only hope that Quandrasi didn't consider them enough of a threat to send any of his goblins after them.

Handri helped Vergil up the stairs, pausing in the hall before the smashed-in front door.

"What is it, Handri?" asked Vergil. "If I don't get to a bed soon, I'm going to collapse on the floor."

"Shh!" Handri hissed. "I think there's someone in the apartment."

Vergil resisted the urge to groan in pain and frustration. He was ready to turn himself in if it meant he could lie down for five minutes.

"Wait here," Handri whispered. Vergil nodded and leaned against the wall while Handri crept into the dark apartment. There was a brief scuffle, followed by a muted yelp from Handri. Vergil forced himself upright and stumbled into the room. He wasn't sure what he could do if Handri had been attacked by goblins, but Handri deserved better than to be deserted. Besides, Vergil didn't have the energy to climb back down the stairs.

"Who goes there?" Vergil demanded—or tried to. His words ran together from exhaustion, so it came out as a barely audible "Huguzzah?"

"You came back!" cried a familiar, booming voice, and Vergil gave a sigh of relief. It was Yurgi.

Handri gasped for breath. "Let… me… go!" he croaked.

"Oh, sorry," said Yurgi. "I get excited sometimes."

Vergil heard Handri collapse on the floor. "I think you broke a rib," he moaned.

"I was just happy to see you guys," said Yurgi. "Did I really hurt you?"

"It's alright, Yurgi," Handri said. "You surprised me a little is all. You may be happy to see us, but we can't see you at all. I'm going to find a light."

Vergil felt his way through the dark to the couch and sank into it while Handri scrounged in the dark for a lantern. He managed to find one and get it lit, then sat down across from Vergil. Yurgi had sat down on the floor, her bad leg stretched out before her.

"I tried to catch those goblins, but they were too fast for me," said Yurgi. "I ran after them for a while, but they escaped into the sewers, where I couldn't follow them. Then I got lost and couldn't find my way back to that big house. So I came back here."

"Well, we're glad you did," said Handri. If any of those CAGE goons show up here, we at least have a fighting chance now." Vergil nodded silently, barely able to stay awake.

"You don't have to worry about them," said Yurgi. "I'll stand watch. I mean, I'll sit watch. I can't stand for very long. Did you find anything out about Marko?"

Vergil bit his lip. Yurgi hadn't heard Quandrasi's plan to publicly execute her boss. Telling her now would probably send her into hysterics. "We're going to try to rescue Marko tomorrow," he said.

"So they still have him? We need to go break him out!"

"There is nothing we can do tonight, Yurgi," said Vergil. "We would be very grateful to have your help tomorrow, but for now we must sleep."

"I can't sleep while Lord Balphry is in prison," Yurgi said.

"You should try to get some sleep as well," said Vergil. "We can sleep in shifts."

Yurgi shook her head. "You sleep. Sometimes ogres stay up for days," she said.

Vergil frowned. He supposed this was true, but he doubted it was any easier for Yurgi to go without sleep than it was for her to go without food. He intended to object, but found that he couldn't find the words through the haze of exhaustion that was enveloping him. Vergil drifted off to sleep.

Seventeen

Vergil was awakened by the sound of bells ringing: first two chimes, then three, then two more. After a few seconds, the sequence repeated itself.

"One hour," said Handri, standing somewhere behind him. Vergil sat up to see Yurgi still sitting on the floor in front of him. She looked tired, but wide awake.

"Until curfew?" asked Vergil, confused. Daylight streamed through the windows; it seemed far too early for a curfew.

"Until the trial," said Handri. "I mean, I assume that's what it's for. That's the mandatory public assembly chime."

Vergil leaped off the couch. "Confound this city's cryptic communication system," he growled. "Why did you not wake me earlier?"

"You said you needed sleep to come up with a plan. I figured you'd wake up when you had it. So?"

Vergil stared at him for a moment, not understanding what Handri was asking.

"Trial?" asked Yurgi.

"They're putting on a show trial for Lord Balphry," said Handri. "Then they're going to ex—"

"Plan!" cried Vergil. "Of course! I have a plan!" Clearing away the cobwebs in his brain, he found that in fact, he had no plan.

"I knew it!" said Handri excitedly. "What do we do?" He and Yurgi looked at him expectantly.

"No time to explain all the details now," said Vergil, thinking quickly. "I'll explain it on the way to the city square."

"What's happening in the city square?" asked Yurgi.

"Oh, you weren't there," said Handri. "Quandrasi is planning a—"

"A demonstration," Vergil interjected. "As I said, I'll explain it on the way over." He could only hope he'd be able to think of something on the way over.

Yurgi shrugged, apparently content that they were finally going to be doing something to free her boss. The three of them made their way to the city square, with Vergil and Handri leading the way and Yurgi limping along behind. Twice they ran into gangs of CAGE goblins, and Vergil was certain they recognized him, but after getting a look at Yurgi, the goblins suddenly found themselves with pressing business elsewhere.

The crowd extended well beyond the square itself, spilling into neighboring streets and alleys. Vergil pressed as far forward as he could, but eventually found himself stymied by a near-solid mass of people. They were a good hundred yards away from the *Unity* statue in the center of the square. Vergil noticed that a raised wooden platform had been set up in front of it. The top of the platform was just above eye-level for the humans. Four black-uniformed goblins, armed with halberds, stood at the corners of the stage, looking menacing.

"We can't even get close to the stage," said Handri. "And you still haven't told us the plan." He leaned over toward Vergil and said, more quietly, "Do you even *have* a plan?" Behind them, Yurgi stood silently looking over the crowd, agape at the vast sea of people.

"Of course I have a plan!" Vergil exclaimed, indignant. "Be quiet and I'll finish working out the details." As he surveyed the crowed, he noticed that it seemed to be largely segregated by race. Most of the audience were humans, but there were several pockets of goblins, particularly toward the area of the city known as Goblintown. The borders of these pockets seemed to be in flux, as arguments and occasionally physical confrontations broke out between goblins and humans. The tension in the crowd was palpable. Except for Yurgi, there were no monsters present other than goblins.

A small figure began to ascend to the platform from a ramp: even from this distance, Vergil could tell by his arrogant swagger and his ever-present staff that it was Grimble. That is, it was Quandrasi in the form of Grimble. Grimble-Quandrasi stepped toward a small podium in the middle of the stage, and spent a few seconds fiddling with some sort of device that was affixed to it. Then he cleared his throat, and the sound was suddenly all around them, followed by a terrible high-pitched squeal.

Vergil cringed, raising his arms in front of his face. "What devilry is this?" he cried, and several people around him turned to look at him. They too had been startled by the sudden sound, but no more than they might be by an unexpected peal of thunder.

"It's the sound system, sir," explained Handri.

"Sound system?" asked Vergil.

"Amplified speakers," said Handri. "New technology. I think it uses zelaznium."

Grimble-Quandrasi began to speak, and his voice seemed to come from everywhere at once. Vergil shuddered at the sound. He understood the rationale for the technology, but it seemed unnatural for someone to be able to speak audibly to several thousand people at a time.

"Greetings, fine citizens of Avaressa!" Grimble-Quandrasi said. Many in the crowd cheered, and a few whistled. "For those who do not know me, my name is Grimble, and I am the acting mayor of Avaressa. I'm afraid Mayor Thameril is currently unavailable, for reasons that I will explain in a moment."

Disapproving mutters and boos arose from the crowd.

"Fortunately I, Grimble, am more than qualified to conduct these proceedings, and I thank you for coming out today to witness this historical event. I imagine you are wondering why I have summoned you here, so please allow me to explain. As I'm sure you all know, there has been some unrest in the city of late, and I have been working tirelessly to get to the bottom of it."

"*You're* at the bottom of it!" somebody not far from Vergil shouted. "Your CAGE goons are riling up the whole city!" Murmurs of assent went up around the man.

It was very unlikely that Grimble-Quandrasi could hear the man, but he went on, "Now I know some of you probably blame the Committee for Advancement of Goblin Equality for the recent troubles, and I will acknowledge that some excesses have occurred."

Grumbling and muttering went up from the crowd, and a few distant people yelled epithets that Vergil couldn't make out.

"Yes, yes, I quite understand your agitation," Grimble-Quandrasi went on. "I have heard your complaints, and I am pleased to announce that I am immediately disbanding CAGE. The organization has served its purpose and is no longer needed."

There were surprised and mostly approving murmurs from the crowd. Vergil was too far from any of the goblin enclaves to judge the reaction there, but he supposed it was somewhat more muted.

"But although CAGE has contributed somewhat to the discord in the city," Grimble-Quandrasi went on, "it is not the root cause of the troubles."

Shouts went up from several goblins. They were too far away for Vergil to make out their words, but he could guess what they were saying—as could Quandrasi, no doubt.

"Indeed," Grimble-Quandrasi continued, "the vigilante group known as KLAMP has also stirred up its share of trouble. In fact, it was largely this group's lawless actions that made CAGE necessary. KLAMP too has been disbanded and its leaders have been imprisoned."

There were cheers from the goblin sections. The reaction from the humans was more ambivalent. When the cheers died down, Grimble-Quandrasi continued:

"But KLAMP was also only a symptom of the root problem. In fact, to some degree I can sympathize with KLAMP's goals. Their members are mostly good men, who thought they were doing what they needed to do in order to save their city. They were misguided and their tactics were unacceptable, but I believe they meant well. You see, fine citizens, *you* are not the problem here. None of you, neither goblins nor humans. You only want the best for yourself and your own kind, as all living creatures do. Occasionally our two races have our differences, but generally we can work out our differences without resorting to violence, which of course none of us wants."

Murmurs of agreement went up from the crowd. Vergil didn't like the way this was going at all. He had expected Quandrasi to launch into an angry tirade in an attempt to rile up the crowd, but he was taking a much more subtle tack, depicting himself as the voice of reason. By disbanding CAGE and expressing sympathy toward KLAMP's members, he was fooling the crowd into believing he had no agenda other than justice and reconciliation.

"What is he up to?" Handri asked. "I thought he said he needed the crowd to be angry."

"They are," said Vergil. As someone who had gone to sleep angry and woke up angry a hundred years later, he knew something about the resilience of anger. "He just needs to redirect their anger. Listen."

Grimble-Quandrasi continued, "Sadly, during the course of my exhaustive investigation of the causes of the recent troubles, I have found that there are those who do not share the goal of living together in peaceful coexistence. Yes, as difficult as it may be for decent citizens like yourselves to believe, there are those among us who actively desire to provoke discord between our races." He paused a moment to allow this remark to settle on the audience. The crowd buzzed and murmured in anticipation. "My investigation led me to one individual in particular," Grimble-Quandrasi went on. "A man who has become obscenely wealthy on the backs of Avaressa's most vulnerable citizens. A man whose quest for wealth and power has left a trail of dead and maimed workers in and around this city. A man who is not even above burning down his own mill to intimidate those demanding better working conditions."

The murmurs of the crowd became louder and more agitated, and Vergil cringed. It had to be clear to most of the crowd that Grimble-Quandrasi was talking about Marko. Marko hadn't been to blame for the fire—not directly, anyway—but Quandrasi obviously had no qualms about twisting the facts to fit his narrative. Vergil wanted to object, but even if Quandrasi heard him—which was unlikely—his protests would accomplish nothing. Vergil would be arrested and either used as a witness against Quandrasi or made to take the blame in Marko's place. His chivalrous instincts told him this would be a noble sacrifice, but the more sensible part of his brain told him it would be pointless: implicating himself wouldn't save Marko; it would only result in Vergil being beheaded alongside him.

A rumbling voice above Vergil startled him; at first he thought it was another glitch in the 'sound system.' It turned out to be Yurgi, bending over to bring her mouth within a few inches of his head. "Who is he talking about?" she asked. "Where is Lord Balphry?"

Vergil had a sickening feeling that they were going to find out where Marko was soon enough, and he still didn't have even the faintest inkling of a plan. Somehow he had to rescue Marko and put an end to this circus before something very bad happened. The situation was troubling enough when he thought the goblins and humans were going to turn on each other en masse, but Quandrasi's rhetoric hinted at something far worse. He was going to try to focus their anger on a single person in order to... how did he put it? "Channel the crowd's hatred into physical form." But what did that mean? How could hatred be channeled into physical form?"

Grimble-Quandrasi continued, "And I have learned that while exploiting the working poor, this man has been bribing city officials—including several members of the city council—to look the other way. It appears that even our respected mayor, Thameril, has received such bribes."

Gasps and murmurs went up from the crowd.

Grimble-Quandrasi held up his hands to silence the crowd. "The city guard attempted to bring Thameril in for questioning, but he left town under the cover of darkness. I have in my possession, however, records documenting these improper payments as well as evidence that Thameril was involved in coordinating the Knights for the Limitation of the Advancement of Monstrous Populations."

More gasps and murmurs.

"Yes, it is a sad day when even our most respected politicians cannot be trusted. But Mayor Thameril too is only a minor figure in this scandal. The true villain in this story is the man who paid those bribes to conceal his illicit activities. And that man's crimes go far beyond the corrupting of city officials and exploiting the poor. I also have in my possession incontrovertible evidence that the man in question has been plotting for some time against the people of this city. I believe his goal was to turn the humans and goblins of Avaressa against each other—to provoke violence and riots in the city, perhaps even to destroy the city itself. He has done this through a wide range of underhanded deals, blackmail, bribes, threats, deception and manipulation. Why did he do this? What was his endgame? To be honest, fellow citizens, I find it difficult to comprehend the motives of such a perverse, malevolent mind. In the end, I believe this man sought nothing more than mayhem and destruction. And he very nearly succeeded in causing this city to turn on itself, destroying it from the inside out as not even the most voracious horde of barbarians could. Fortunately, I was able to uncover this dastardly plot before it got to that point. The culprit has been apprehended, and will now stand trial for his wicked deeds before you. Ladies and gentlemen, I present to you this scheming malefactor, this oozing pustule on the body politic of this fine city, the foul villain himself—"

"Lord Balphry!" Yurgi suddenly roared, so loudly that even Grimble-Quandrasi heard her. He broke off in mid-sentence and peered into the crowd, his eyes alighting on the lone ogre. All around Vergil and Handri, heads turned to gape at Yurgi.

Yurgi's eyes were fixed on a procession that was making its way through the crowd, perhaps a stone's throw away. Following her gaze, Vergil caught a glimpse of a metal cage being wheeled across the square. Several members of the city guard were in front of it and behind it. He couldn't make out the features of the man in the cage, but there was only one person it could be.

"I'm coming, Lord Balphry!" Yurgi bellowed, and began to plod through the crowd toward the cage. Terrified, people backed out of her way, leaving a wide passage.

"Come on!" yelled Vergil, following close behind her.

"Is this part of your plan?" asked Handri.

"Eh?" said Vergil. "Yes, of course. Just try to keep up!"

Yurgi had picked up speed, and was now lumbering along at a considerable pace, swinging her injured leg out in front of her as she ran. Vergil and Handri had to sprint to stay with her. Then suddenly she stopped, and Vergil ran smack into the back of her leg. A split second later, Handri ran into him, and the two of them fell backwards, collapsing on the pavement. Dazed, Vergil lay on the ground watching Yurgi straining to pull apart the bars of a cage that was just big enough to fit a man. Inside, Marko watched her, his face a mix of hope and terror. Guards were streaming around the cage from both the front and back, their short swords drawn.

Vergil struggled to his knees, trying to get to Yurgi in time to help her—although it wasn't clear what he could do, as he was unarmed and still had no plan to speak of. Handri had pulled himself to his feet next to him, and helped Vergil up. When Vergil made to move toward Yurgi, though, Handri put a hand on his chest to stop him.

Meanwhile Yurgi, having noticed the guards swarming around her, stopped trying to bend the bars and put her back to the cage. Vergil saw that she had bent the bars a fair amount, perhaps just enough for Marko to climb out. Marko, however, was not looking inclined to escape at the moment. Yurgi was turning first to her left and then to her right, snarling at the guards as they threatened her with their swords.

Finally one of them was brave enough to take a jab at her injured knee. His blade penetrated the bandage just above the knee, causing Yurgi to wince in pain. But before he could withdraw the blade, Yurgi bent over, clutching the guard around his left thigh with her massive hand. She picked him up and spun around, hurling him at three other guards who were approaching from behind. Two of the guards went sprawling to the pavement while the third slammed into the side of the cage.

Guards continued to pour around both sides of the cage toward Yurgi—more than could possibly have been needed to roll the cage to the stage. Some of them seemed to emerge from the crowd, as if they had been waiting for this moment. Suddenly there was a ring of at least twenty of them around Yurgi, and still more men continued to filter out of the crowd.

"It's a trap!" Vergil gasped, and several people turned to stare at him. The guards, however, took no notice, as they were preoccupied with subduing Yurgi.

"Please, sir," Handri urged. "There is nothing we can do."

Vergil watched helplessly as the guards continued to swarm around Yurgi. One of them sliced at her calf with his sword while another hacked at her knee with a halberd. A third had climbed onto Marko's cage and leaped onto Yurgi's shoulder, jabbing a dagger into her neck. Yurgi howled and slapped the man off, sending him flying into the crowd. She gave the man with the halberd a kick, knocking him backwards into two of his fellows, and the three of them sprawled onto their backs. Then she spun around, pounding the slicer on the head with her fist. He fell limply to the ground.

But for every man she took down, two more seemed to appear, and they gradually formed a tighter and tighter ring around her. Already Yurgi was bleeding badly, and it was clear that she was having trouble standing on her bad leg. She glanced toward Vergil briefly as if to plead for help, but then turned her attention back to the fracas. He saw her toss aside six more men before they she fell. Then the crowd converged in front of Vergil again, and she was lost from view. One of the guards was looking their direction.

"We should get out of here," said Handri.

Vergil nodded reluctantly, allowing Handri to guide him away from the scene. Soon they were once again lost in a sea of spectators. Handri was right: there was nothing they could do for Yurgi. Vergil had failed to come up with any sort of plan, and because of his failure Yurgi too was going to die.

"I apologize for the delay," said Grimble-Quandrasi's voice, from all around them. "For those who couldn't see, we had a bit of excitement over here, but everything is under control now. One of the accused's former employees attempted to interfere with the proceedings, but this was anticipated and has been taken care of."

As he spoke, Yurgi's head came into view over the crowd. She was being prodded up the ramp by the guards. It soon became evident that her hands were shackled. A guard with a halberd jabbed her in the ribs and she fell to the floor of the stage. One of the guards secured one end of a chain to her shackles; the other end seemed to be connected to the stage. It did indeed appear Quandrasi had been prepared for Yurgi's interference. Vergil cursed his stupidity; he should never have let Yurgi get near Quandrasi's assembly. The men moved out of the way and several more appeared on the stage, pulling Marko's cage onto the stage with them.

"This," Grimble-Quandrasi said, pointing at Yurgi, "is the employee in question. The poor dumb brute has actually convinced herself that the accused cares about her, when in fact he would sacrifice her as willingly as he's betrayed the rest of us." Even from this distance, Yurgi looked sullen and defeated, and next to the three-story-tall statue of *Unity*, she also looked downright tiny. The statue, its huge arms extended in front of it, looked like was about to reach out and tear Yurgi in half. Vergil shook his head, irritated with himself at the thought. Why was he occupying his mind with facile notions of statues coming alive when—

Suddenly panic set in. The crowd seemed to be closing in all around him, and there was no escape. Vergil's heart pounded in his chest and it became very difficult to breathe. Light-headed, he stumbled into Handri, who caught him before he collapsed to the pavement.

"Sir!" cried Handri. "What is wrong? Can you breathe?"

"You," Vergil gasped. "You!"

Handri stared at him, uncomprehending.

Meanwhile, Grimble-Quandrasi had walked over to Marko's cage, where Marko stood quaking with fear, his face clearly visible through the hole Yurgi had made in the cage. "And this, fine citizens of Avaressa," Grimble-Quandrasi was saying, "is the villain himself, the man responsible for all our recent troubles, the one who tried to turn us against each other purely for his own sick, twisted amusement. Ladies and gentlemen, I give you the loathsome scoundrel Marko Milkaduk, also known as Lord Balphry!"

The crowd howled and booed. Some people threw vegetables, which they had apparently been carrying in case this eventuality arose. Handri was doing his best to keep Vergil upright, but gradually failing. "Please, everyone," he pleaded, "give him some room." A few of the onlookers begrudgingly gave up a few inches, allowing Handri to let Vergil sink to a sitting position. Vergil's eyelids fluttered, and his head lolled from side to side and he struggled to remain conscious. "Sir!" cried Handri. "Stay with me!"

"You…" Vergil murmured again, his eyes fixed on Handri, who stared back in bewilderment.

Grimble-Quandrasi's voice continued to boom all around them, hurling slander and depredations at Marko. The crowd ate it up, thrilled to have an object for their pent-up hatred. It was not, after all, each other that they hated, but *this man*. This man who had schemed against them, exploited them, preyed upon them. This man was the source of all the evil and suffering they had experienced over the past days, weeks, maybe even years. Who knew how far back his evil plotting went? This man needed to face justice, to reap the whirlwind he had sown.

"Sir!" cried Handri again, looking as if he were about to burst into tears. "What is it? Have I done something wrong? What do I do?"

"You," Vergil gasped again. He took a deep breath and tried again. "You... ni... tee."

"Unity?" asked Handri, confused. He thought for a moment, and realization came across his face. "You mean the... oh. Oh, no. You don't think the statue is the...."

"It's the... golem," gasped Vergil. Feeling the solidity of the pavement under his palms, he forced himself to slow down and take a deep breath. "The mythical terror of your youth. The shadowy figure of my nightmares."

"No," said Handri, shaking his head. "No, it can't be."

"Hatred made incarnate," Vergil gasped. "The creature that will devour all of Dis!"

Eighteen

While Handri absorbed Vergil's revelation about the golem, Vergil closed his eyes and forced himself to take several deep, slow breaths. Meanwhile, Grimble-Quandrasi continued to stoke the crowd's revulsion toward Marko, blaming him for everything from a sanitation workers' strike to the past year's poor cucumber crop. The worst of Vergil's panic eventually subsided, and he got shakily to his feet, leaning heavily on Handri.

Still Grimble-Quandrasi continued to spew his hate. So compelling was Quandrasi's rhetoric that even Vergil, who knew better, felt his anger against Marko rekindling in his chest. Marko was, after all, the man who had neglected Vergil's care during his slumber, nearly causing him to lose a leg. It was Marko who had stolen his money and sent him on a fool's errand to distract him from Marko's own embezzlement. And it was Marko who had set in motion the events that had greatly accelerated Quandrasi's scheme. If it weren't for his manipulation of Vergil, the situation in the city would not yet be so desperate, and there would still be time to put an end to the madness. And who would miss Marko, anyway? What good did he ever contribute to the world? If one greedy old aristocrat needed to die to pacify the city, then wasn't it worth it?

But Vergil shook his head, forcing this thought away. Marko didn't deserve to die—and even if he did, his death wouldn't solve the problem. The problem was the seething, irrational hatred of the populace. Adding to that hatred would do nothing but distract him from finding a real solution. But what solution was there to blind, mass hatred, other than getting as far away from it as possible? Grimble-Quandrasi was still ranting, but the crowd had begun to chant now, drowning him out. A simple, but blood-curdling chant: *Kill him, kill him, kill him…* The goblins were moving to the center of the stage a device the likes of which Vergil had never seen: a sturdy wooden frame with a heavy steel blade suspended by a rope at the top of it. It wasn't difficult to guess the purpose of this particular machine.

Vergil and Handri stood helplessly, drowning in an undulating sea of hatred and anger. As the chant's volume increased, Vergil imagined he could feel the hatred coming into being, a sort of miasma arising from the crowd and drifting toward Marko. Yurgi looked around the crowd helplessly as Marko stood in his cage, his quaking visible even at this distance. Was it possible for people to kill a man simply by hating him? Vergil was afraid he was soon going to find out.

Grimble-Quandrasi continued to shriek lies and insults about Marko, but he was all but inaudible over the crowd. As their agitation increased, they closed in on the stage, and Vergil and Handri felt themselves crushed together. Vergil's panic started to set in again, and he forced himself to close his eyes and breathe deeply. It was all he could do to block out the deafening chants and the impending sensation of being crushed alive.

Then, suddenly, there was a change in the demeanor of the crowd, one that Vergil could sense even with his eyes clamped shut. The agitation seemed to shift into a sort of expectant calm, and a split second later the chants gave way to an eerie silence—the kind of silence that Vergil would have thought impossible in a city square filled with thousands of people and goblins. And then: panic.

Not the quiet, falling-down-on-the-pavement kind of panic that Vergil had experienced a moment earlier, either. This was full-fledged, all-pervasive terror. It started with a single scream, and then many more, until the air was filled with a piercing cacophony. People began to move—or tried to, anyway. Mostly they ran into each other, trying desperately to put distance between themselves and the thing of Vergil's nightmares.

The statue had *moved*.

First just its left arm—that was what provoked the first scream. When the thing's head cocked slowly to the side, as if to get a better look at the crowd, that was when the terror fully took hold. And Vergil knew that this wasn't terror borne of ignorance, like a child's fear of thunder. No, this fear arose from a terrible knowledge: the people of Avaressa *knew* what they had done. They saw their own hatred in the golem, reflected back to them as in a mirror. And they were afraid.

After the initial confusion, the crowd began to move away from the stage. All around Vergil and Handri, people began to push and shove, screaming and jostling their way past them. Vergil and Handri found themselves hugging each other tightly to avoid being knocked over and trampled. Venturing a glance in the direction of the stage, Vergil saw that the golem had craned its head as if to look down at Marko's cage, seeming to sense something of interest. Of course, thought Vergil. As the object of the hatred that had brought the golem into being, Marko would be the first target of its wrath. But what would it do after Marko was dead? Would its rage be sated, or would it continue to grow? Vergil was afraid he knew the answer.

He and Handri were buffeted for some time by elbows, shoulders, and the occasional fist as the panicked crowd continued to disperse. Several times someone ran headlong into them, nearly bowling them over, but by huddling close together and bending with the blows like a tree in the wind, they remained standing. Finally, the crowd thinned enough that they were out of immediate danger. Releasing Handri, Vergil ventured another look at the golem. He was horrified to see that the golem had clamped its stony hands on either side of Marko's cage. Marko, still inside, braced himself as the cage tilted and moved upward. The golem didn't seem to have fingers; its hands were just mitten-like appendages. It lifted the cage toward its blank face as if to—what? Look at it? Smell it? Whatever senses the golem had, they apparently didn't depend on any identifiable facial features. Vergil found himself shuddering with renewed disgust at the thing. It had been horrific enough when it hadn't been able to move.

The crowd had continued to disperse, and now Vergil and Handri were alone except for a few stragglers, most of whom seemed to be goblins. Grimble-Quandrasi watched the golem gleefully. The black-uniformed guards gaped in amazement at the golem but did not flee; presumably Quandrasi had given them some warning of his plan. Yurgi stood in her shackles, dazed and frightened. Screams and shouts could still be heard, but they were more distant. The golem held the cage close to its face for some time, apparently employing its mysterious senses to appraise the contents. Fortunately for Marko, the gap in the bars Yurgi had made was now facing the ground, uncovered by the golem's hand. He had gotten his legs through it, and as the golem conducted its slow appraisal of the cage, he was gradually shimmying the rest of the way though. It was unclear whether Marko's broad chest and shoulders would fit through the gap, or whether he would be able to get through before the golem finished its inspection and decided to crush the cage or throw it halfway across the city. Vergil had no doubt it was capable of either.

It opted for crushing. Its pushed its massive hands together, bending the bars of the cage like blades of grass. The pressure on the cage momentarily caused the gap to bow slightly wider, however, and suddenly Marko slipped the rest of the way through, barely managing to grasp one of the bars to keep from falling to the pavement below. As the golem continued to squeeze, though, it became clear that if Vergil didn't let go soon, he'd never be able to. He released his grip as the cage collapsed in the golem's hand, falling a good two stories to the ground. Vergil heard a crack as he hit, and Marko let out a howl of pain.

The golem didn't react to the scream, but it suddenly lost interest in the cage, tossing it aside like an empty can. Somehow, despite its lack of eyes, nose and mouth, it knew Marko was no longer inside. It rotated its head first to the left, then to the right, and then craned its neck downward. Marko's right leg appeared to be broken, but he was doing his best not to move or make a sound. It didn't make any difference. The golem somehow pinpointed Marko's location and reached out for him with its right hand. Seeing the massive hand moving toward him, Marko began to drag himself out of the way, but it was clear he wasn't going to get far.

"Stop!" cried Vergil, without thinking. "It's not his fault!"

"What are you doing, sir?" Handri gasped. "You can't stop that thing!"

"I have to try, Handri. I am still a knight, after all. Marko may be a scoundrel, but he does not deserve to die, particularly at the hands of that thing. If those are indeed hands. Give my love to—" He stopped, realizing he had no friends in Dis but Handri. He smiled grimly. "Goodbye, friend," he said, and ran toward the golem.

Vergil reached Marko a few seconds before the golem's hand blotted out the sun above them. Vergil got behind Marko and knelt down, putting his arms under Marko's armpits and clutching him around the chest. With a mighty exertion, he managed to pull Marko out of the way just as the golem's open palm slammed down on the concrete. Marko screamed; his leg dragged behind him, his toes pointing in completely the wrong direction. A ragged end of bone protruded from a tear in his bloody pant leg.

"I'm sorry, Marko," said Vergil, "but I need to get you away from that thing."

Marko nodded, but he was grimacing in pain. Tears rolled down his cheeks.

Grimble-Quandrasi had moved to the edge of the stage to leer excitedly at them. "Crush them!" he squealed, raising his staff over his head. "Crush them both!" To his right, Yurgi struggled vainly at her chains.

Lacking the strength to lift Marko bodily, Vergil shuffled backwards, awkwardly dragging Marko with him. Marko did his best not to scream, but Vergil wasn't sure it made any difference. Somehow the golem knew where they were. It straightened up, took a tentative step forward, trying out its new legs, and then reached down to grab them again. Its hand had almost reached them when it stopped, as if distracted by something. A moment later, Vergil heard a halting voice: "O-over here, y-you big pile of r-rocks!"

Vergil turned to see Handri, shaking like a newborn foal, standing not far away.

"Handri, you fool!" cried Vergil. "Get out of here!"

But Handri's plan to distract the golem seemed to be working. The golem turned its face toward Handri, then back to Marko and Vergil, and then again to Handri. It took a step toward Handri and bent down toward him. The golem's face was nearly as tall as Handri.

"Run, Handri!" Vergil shouted. But Handri stood his ground, his face gone completely pale. At the last second, when the golem's hand was about to clamp shut on him, he turned and darted out of the way.

Vergil, meanwhile, continued to drag Marko, who had given up his effort to resist screaming. No matter how loudly Marko screamed, though, the golem's attention remained fixed on Handri, who was darting back and forth across the square, dodging the golem as it stomped after him, each of its footsteps like a crack of thunder. So far, Handri had been able to stay free of the golem's clutches, but the creature seemed to getting faster as it pursued him, learning how to use its new limbs as it went along. Handri wouldn't be able to stay ahead of it for long, and Vergil was near exhaustion just from dragging Marko a few yards through the square. There was no conceivable way he'd be able to get Marko out of harm's way in time.

Grimble-Quandrasi cackled at them from the stage, his shrill, rasping laugh coming from everywhere at once. "Run all you want, fools!" he shrieked. "There is no escape from the Hate Golem! Give in to your fear!"

At Quandrasi's words, revelation dawned on Vergil. He knew now why the golem had gone after Handri, even before Handri had begun shouting at it. It wasn't sight, sound, or even scent that attracted the golem. "Handri!" Vergil cried, as Handri dived out of the way. "It senses your fear!" The golem's fist came crashing down on the pavement.

"I'm not surprised!" Handri shouted back. "I've got more than enough of it!"

"No, don't you understand? It has no other senses! It can only see you because of your fear! All you have to do is stop being afraid, and it won't attack you!" A glance at Grimble-Quandrasi confirmed his hypothesis: the goblin was scowling at him, irritated that he'd said too much.

"If it would stop attacking me," shouted Handri, gasping for breath, "I would stop being afraid!"

The golem's foot came down with a crash, Handri diving out of the way without a second to spare. Handri was drenched in sweat and clearly spent; he was soon going to collapse. He got to his feet and staggered away as the golem bent down and reached toward him. Its hand closed, and for a moment Vergil was certain Handri would be crushed. Handri gave a yelp as the creature's appendages clamped shut just behind him. He didn't appear injured, but he wasn't moving forward either. Vergil realized after a moment that the golem had gotten hold of the back of Handri's shirt. The golem hesitated, apparently confused regarding what to do about this, and by the time it decided to lift Handri up by his shirt, he was already halfway out of it. He squirmed and wriggled as the massive hand pulled him upwards, the shirt having slipped over his head. When he was a few feet in the air, the shirt tore and he fell out of it, landing on his feet and tumbling to the ground. This puzzled the golem, but after a moment it let the shirt go and craned its head back toward Handri. Handri, seemingly uninjured, got to his feet and scurried away. The golem took a step toward him, nearly crushing him with its amorphous foot, which was the size of a horse. It cracked the pavement, cantilevering shards of concrete at all angles. Handri lost his footing on the shifting ground and sprawled to the ground face-first. He got to his knees, dazed.

"Trust me, Handri!" Vergil called, desperately hoping he was right. "Stand still and face the golem. And don't be afraid!"

Handri looked at Vergil, then looked down at the ground. He took a deep breath, closed his eyes, and then stood up. He turned around and faced the golem, pointing his chin at its face and puffing his bare chest out—which had the unfortunate effect of making look even more simian than usual. His hand shook at his side.

"Don't be afraid!" Vergil yelled.

"I'm not!" shouted Handri.

"Yes, you are!" Vergil yelled. "I can see your hand shaking!"

"I'm cold!" yelled Handri. "That thing took my shirt!"

The golem was bending over toward him, its blank face moving this way and that, trying to determine where Handri had gone.

"It's a phantom, Handri," Vergil called. "Just a bogeyman from your childhood. It has no power over you."

Handri nodded, but his hand still shook. The golem's face was pointed directly at Handri, and its outstretched hand was moving toward him. Just before it reached him, Handri turned and staggered away. The hand clamped shut, nearly crushing him. Handri was limping; he seemed to have hurt himself in the fall.

"I can't do it!" Handri yelled. "It's going to kill me!"

"No, it isn't!" Vergil shouted. "It's just a mindless thing! It's not even really alive. It's just a sort of soulless machine, like..." He tried to think of something Handri wouldn't be afraid of. "A train! It's like the train you saved me from!"

"You don't stand in front of trains!" Handri cried. The golem's foot came crashing down a few feet away from him.

"It's not *exactly* like a train. But you know how it works now. It runs on a track. That track is your fear. Just redirect your fear. Make the track go around you."

"Make the track go around me?" said Handri.

"Yes!" Vergil yelled. "Let go of it. Let it pass around you. When it's gone, only you will remain."

Handri nodded, closing his eyes. "Fear is a train track," he said. "Make it go around me."

The golem craned its head forward, trying to locate Handri. Handri stood stock still except for his left hand, which still quivered. The golem's head pivoted left, then right, then left again, slowly pinpointing his location. Vergil saw Handri's lips moving and realized he was murmuring "Fear is a train track. Make it go around me," over and over. Hearing the words, Vergil glanced at Marko, who was lying on the pavement next to him. Marko was murmuring the mantra as well, and Vergil found himself mimicking them. "Fear is a train track," he said. "Make it go around me."

The golem leaned forward, and Vergil winced as the massive, flat face moved toward Handri. He was certain the golem's head was going to bowl him over. But the golem's face stopped a few inches from Handri, and Handri remained standing, oblivious, his eyes still closed. Vergil silently prayed that he didn't open his eyes; if he did, he'd be startled out of his wits—and his fear would bring his doom.

But Handri simply stood with his eyes closed, repeating his mantra. Vergil saw that his hand had stopped shaking. He stood perfectly still, his face calm, as if he were listening to the sound of waves on a beach. The golem continued to loom over him, but made no move. Finally it straightened up, turning its head to the right, and stomped away.

When the sound of the creature's steps began to diminish, Handri opened his eyes, watching in awe as the thing lumbered away. "Fear *is* a train track!" he exclaimed. "I did it, sir!"

"You did indeed, friend," said Vergil. "Now help me get Marko away from here!"

Handri ran over to them. They put Marko's arms around their necks—Vergil on the left, Handri on the right—and carried him to the edge of the square. A young goblin boy stared at them from around the corner.

"You there! Young goblin!" said Vergil. He took his last silver piece from his pocket and held it up. "Get a bottle of whiskey from that tavern."

The goblin ran to him, grabbed the silver, and darted off toward the tavern. Marko groaned in pain. His face was white and his skin had gone clammy. "Hang on, Marko," said Vergil. "We'll find a doctor to look at that leg soon." Unless we're all dead, he thought. He looked across the square toward the golem, which was lumbering toward the stage. The square was now completely deserted except for a score or so goblins who had assembled near the stage. The fact that they all seemed to be armed—and hadn't fled from the gigantic stone monster—suggested they had been warned in advance. Vergil noticed that the goblin with the eye patch was among them. So much for disbanding CAGE; it seemed that Quandrasi had simply been keeping his thugs in reserve until he needed them. But that wasn't Vergil's primary concern at the moment.

"Oh, no," said Handri, following his gaze. "Yurgi."

Yurgi was crouched on the stage, watching the golem approach. Even from this distance, her fear was evident. The golem had "seen" her.

The young goblin returned with a bottle of whiskey, which Vergil held up to Marko's mouth. He took several gulps, then coughed violently. The coughing was followed by a pained moan.

"We have to warn her," said Handri.

"You're injured," replied Vergil. Handri was standing on his left foot and leaning against the wall. Vergil handed Handri the whiskey. "Stay with Marko."

Handri nodded, taking the bottle and sitting down next to Marko.

Vergil set off running across the square. He pushed himself as fast as his sore muscles and tired joints would let him, but it was clear he would never make it in time to warn Yurgi. The golem was almost upon her. She was standing now, straining impotently at her chains. The goblin guards on the stage were backing away from her. If they were afraid too, their fear was outweighed by their confidence that the golem was only interested in Yurgi. Grimble-Quandrasi stood only a few paces from Yurgi, grinning maniacally as the golem approached, holding out his staff in front of him. Vergil wondered how Quandrasi could be so confident the golem wouldn't accidentally crush him while going after Yurgi. The CAGE goons had backed well away to the side of the stage.

"Yurgi!" Vergil gasped as he approached. "Fear!"

Yurgi glanced at him in confusion, still straining against her chains. Vergil hoped Yurgi hadn't heard him, because he was giving her the opposite message of what he had intended.

Grimble-Quandrasi scowled momentarily at Vergil as he approached, but then turned his attention back to the golem. He backed away a few steps, still holding the staff in front of him.

The staff, thought Vergil. The globe at the tip of his staff wasn't made from silver: it was zelaznium. Somehow he was using it to communicate with the golem. It wasn't clear what that communication consisted of; he seemed to have been unable to compel the golem to attack Handri. Maybe all it did was keep the golem from attacking him. But there was definitely a connection between the staff and the golem, and that made Vergil wonder how deep the connection went.

The golem was now standing just a few feet from the stage, and it was reaching down with both hands to grab Yurgi. Yurgi had the chain wrapped around her forehand to eliminate the slack, and was standing with both knees bent, pulling with all her might. She had to be in excruciating pain from her injured knee, but she didn't show it. Every muscle in her body strained as she tried to break the chain. For a sickening moment the golem held its hands outstretched, one on either side of Yurgi. Then it brought them together in a clap, sending the sound of stone-against-stone echoing through the square.

Nineteen

"No!" cried Vergil, falling to his knees on the pavement. This was his fault. Poor, stupid, innocent Yurgi's death was his fault.

But as the golem spread its arms again, Vergil saw that its hands were empty. Yurgi had torn the chain free, and was sitting, dazed, toward the rear of the stage, still clutching the chain in her hands. At the end of it was a section of the stage, larger than she was, that had broken loose. The golem seemed aware that its prey had escaped; it reached across the stage with its right hand, knocking two of the goblins clear off the stage in the process. The golem formed a fist and brought it down on the stage to crush Yurgi. But Yurgi dived out of the way, dragging the section of stage behind her. The golem's fist smashed the section into thousands of fragments. Yurgi got up and limped away.

"Yurgi, the staff!" Vergil yelled, struggling to his feet. "Get the staff!"

Yurgi looked at Vergil and then at Grimble-Quandrasi, who stood a few feet from her. Yurgi took a step toward him, and he quailed and ran to the ramp at edge of the stage. "Stop her!" Grimble-Quandrasi cried, as he passed the two remaining black-uniformed goblins on the stage. The two goblins glanced uncertainly at each other, then turned to face Yurgi, leveling the points of their halberds in her direction. Yurgi snarled, drawing her chain back behind her and then whipping in front of her. The chain missed the goblins but swept right through the halberd shafts, severing the heads and sending them clattering to the stage. The goblins, left holding useless splintered poles, dropped them and ran after their boss.

But while Yurgi had been distracted by the goblins, the golem had pivoted and was again reaching out with its huge fist. The fist hung for a second over Yurgi's head, and Vergil knew that this time she would not escape. Rather than attack Yurgi, though, the golem extended its arm until its fist was over the two goblins scurrying down the ramp, then slammed it down hard, crushing them both. Vergil grimaced and looked away as the two broken goblin corpses slid down the bloody ramp. The golem pulled its arm back and turned to face Yurgi again.

Vergil had moved to the edge of the stage. "Yurgi," he called, "it can sense your—"

But Yurgi was paying no attention. She had gathered the chain up and hobbled to the edge of the stage. She stepped onto the pavement, wincing as the weight landed on her bad knee. While the golem tried to find her again, Yurgi limped to the golem's left foot.

"What are you doing, Yurgi?" asked Vergil. "You can't—"

Yurgi had drawn the chain behind her back again, and then whipped it forward, bringing it down on the golem's foot with a deafening crack. The stone surface cracked, and Vergil ducked and held up his arms as shards went flying. The damage appeared minimal, though; Yurgi was going to have to either hit the golem many more times to do any real harm. Judging from the look on her face, that was exactly what she intended to do. Vergil backed away as she drew the chain behind her again. She brought it down again, even harder, widening the crack and breaking of several more shards of stone. Vergil started to suspect that she might actually be able to take the giant down: if she could hobble the golem, they might have a chance to defeat it. Then the golem kicked her.

It was more of a gradual sweeping motion than a true kick, but the golem's toe caught Yurgi in the gut, lifting her up and catapulting her across the square. She landed on the roof of a tanner's shop, collapsing it and disappearing in a cloud of dust. She didn't get up.

Vergil felt his fear creeping back—fear not for himself, but for the people of Avaress. With Yurgi out of action, there was nothing between the golem and total destruction of the city. He considered giving in to the fear so that the golem would attack him instead, but all that would only delay the mayhem by a few seconds. He pushed the fear away, and the golem ignored him, turning instead toward Grimble-Quandrasi, who now stood flanked by the two guards who remained mostly intact.

"Go, mighty colossus!" Grimble-Quandrasi shrieked, waving his staff at the golem. "Destroy as you were created to do!"

The golem turned and began to stomp its way across the square to toward the city.

Vergil darted toward Grimble-Quandrasi, managing to grab the staff before the goblins could react. But he was too weak to pry it from the illusionist's hands, and one of the goblins jabbed him in the ribs with the butt of his halberd, knocking Vergil to the ground.

"Foolish old man," Grimble-Quandrasi crowed. "A relic of another time. Tell me, Sir Vergil, how are your quaint notions of chivalry and decency serving you? Haven't you learned yet that there is no place for kindness or forgiveness in this new world. This is a time of steam and steel!"

The CAGE goons, having evidently decided the safest spot in the city was near Grimble, had gathered around him, their hands on their swords.

"Why are you doing this?" Vergil gasped, clutching his side. "You cannot possibly control that thing!"

"I never intended to control it," said Grimble-Quandrasi. "Don't you see? Order is an aberration, love an anomaly. I have seen through the illusion that is civilization, and behind it there is nothing but chaos. We are all fools dancing at the edge of an abyss, and now the eyes of all races will be opened to that truth!"

"You are mad," said Vergil. It was not so much an accusation as a revelation. Up to this point, he had assumed that there was some grand vision behind Quandrasi's plan; that he intended to rule over a new goblin kingdom in Dis or to profit in some other way from the destruction. But it wasn't so. Quandrasi craved only destruction, and there seemed to be no way to stop him. The golem would lay waste to Avaress and then seek out terror wherever it could find it. Perhaps eventually the rulers of Dis could unite to defeat the golem, but how many thousands would die before then? Perhaps if Vergil could get the word out about how to resist the golem, the people might have a chance, but there was no time: nothing traveled faster than fear.

"Sanity is an illusion," said Grimble-Quandrasi.

"Don't you see what he's doing?" Vergil said, turning to one guard and then the other. "He has no interest in goblin rights. He wants to destroy all of civilization!"

The goblins shrugged. "Humans got a lot more to lose than goblins," said one of them. The other nodded.

"But that's..." Vergil started, then realized he had no idea how to respond to this argument. It was true; with a more advanced civilization, humans had more to lose. And if that's all these goblins cared about, there wasn't anything he could say to change their minds. He sighed, turning to watch the golem stomp toward the most populous part of the city. In the distance, he could hear the screams of people who were watching from windows and doorways. Soon their houses and shops would be rubble, and many of them would die, and there was nothing Vergil could do about it.

The golem had reached the edge of the square, marching right past Handri and Marko. Vergil sat helplessly on the ground as Grimble-Quandrasi, flanked by his two goblin guards, watching gleefully as the creature advanced.

And then it tripped.

Vergil didn't believe his eyes at first, but he couldn't imagine why Quandrasi would effect such an illusion. The golem had just passed the the first row of buildings when it suddenly fell flat on its face with a tremendous crash. A glance at Grimble-Quandrasi confirmed Vergil wasn't imagining it: the goblin-illusionist looked furious.

"Blast you, you worthless slab of granite," Grimble-Quandrasi snarled, "get up!" He took off running across the square, his entourage of goblins following closely behind. Vergil got to his feet and went after them.

Soon Vergil saw the cause: the golem had fallen victim to the same trick Lagorna had pulled on the CAGE goons who had been chasing him and Handri. A very thick rope, braided together from slimmer cords, had been pulled taut across the street the golem had entered. Several dozen goblins had evidently offered themselves up as bait, luring the golem down that street, and then darted out of the way when the golem fell. At least, Vergil hoped they had all gotten out of the way. These goblins, along with dozens of others, had begun swarming all over the golem's fallen form, in an apparent effort to pin the creature down. Vergil didn't see Lagorna among them, but he had no doubt she was behind this. She hadn't fled town after all.

"Get up!" cried Grimble-Quandrasi again, as he approached the feet of the fallen golem. He waved his staff at it, and the creature stirred. Goblins continued to pour out of the alleys, climbing on top of the golem. "Get up!" Grimble-Quandrasi shrieked again.

For a moment, Vergil considered making another grab for Quandrasi's staff, but the two guards with the halberds still flanked the illusionist, and the CAGE goons were forming a rough circle around him. There was no way Vergil would get to him.

Lacking any other ideas, he ran past Quandrasi's entourage to join the rapidly growing group that was weighing down the golem. But as he neared the golem's ankle, the creature's leg twitched, knocking him backwards against a wall. He struck his head on the brick and fell to the ground, stunned. A few goblins were thrown off, but goblins were fast and agile climbers, and many more of them continue to spill out of the alleys to climb on top of the golem. On the golem's back, they were now stacked three and four deep in some places. Would it be enough to keep it down? And what would they do if they succeeded? Take shifts on its back until they could chain the thing down?

Glancing at Grimble-Quandrasi, Vergil saw that he was leaning on his staff and sweating profusely, his eyes fixed on the golem. He closed his eyes and murmured inaudibly. Then, with great effort, he lift his staff and brought it down hard on the concrete. The golem's body jerked in response, as if energy had been transmitted to it through the pavement. The golem managed to raise its head, despite the sixteen goblins currently perched on it. Slowly and haltingly the golem began to rise. The goblins on its head and back shrieked and howled as they lost their grip, tumbling and striking other goblins on the way down. Many of them rolled down to its legs or fell to the street, and as the burdened lightened, the golem moved with more ease. In the street, goblins screamed and ran in all directions. They had nearly stopped the golem, but Quandrasi had somehow managed to impart enough strength to the golem to foil their trap. If only Vergil could get Quandrasi's staff away from him, he might still stop it—but what chance did he have? Even if Vergil could rally the goblins, there was no way such a ragtag band could fight their way through the CAGE goons.

But as Vergil turned to look at Grimble-Quandrasi, he saw that something strange was happening. The air had begun to shimmer around Grimble-Quandrasi, the way it had when the illusionist had transformed in the past. Grimble-Quandrasi leaned with both hands on his staff, looking like he was about to fall over. His eyes were closed and he swayed like a drunken man. As the shimmering intensified, Vergil realized what had happened. The golem derived its strength from Quandrasi, channeled through the staff, and Quandrasi had exerted so much effort prodding the golem to its feet that he'd lost control over his illusion. Vergil pulled himself to his feet.

As the golem stood up, Quandrasi opened his eyes, breathing a sigh of relief. But a moment later a look of concern came over his face as he noticed that the members of his goblin entourage were now staring open-mouthed at him. For it was no longer their leader, Grimble, who stood before them, but a strange old man in a blue robe. Quandrasi looked down at his robe and then back at the goblins. "Okay," he croaked, his voice barely above a whisper, holding his hand. "I can explain."

As the goblins continued to stare at Quandrasi, Vergil walked toward them.

"You're not Grimble," said the goblin with the eye patch. The two guards with the halberds glanced at each other nervously, reassessing their allegiances.

"No," admitted Quandrasi. "I am not. But I'm continuing Grimble's work. I have sent the Hate Golem into the human part of the city to tear it down, so that goblins can finally have their chance at rule!"

But the golem had been apprising its situation and, having apparently decided that there were no longer any good targets in the vicinity, turned around and began to stomp back toward the square. Quandrasi smiled weakly at them.

"That thing doesn't care who it kills," said a familiar voice behind Vergil. Vergil turned to see Lagorna striding toward Quandrasi. "It will destroy your homes and kill your families and friends. That's exactly what Quandrasi wants."

"How do we stop it?" asked the goblin with the eye patch.

"Take the staff," said Vergil.

"No!" cried Quandrasi. "You don't know how to control it! You don't know what will happen!"

"I have a pretty good idea," said Vergil. He nodded to Lagorna, who took a step toward Quandrasi and held out her hands.

"You'll never take me alive!" Quandrasi shouted, and suddenly purple smoke billowed up from around his feet. For several seconds, the whole group was blind. Then the breeze carried the smoke away, revealing that Quandrasi hadn't moved. The goblin guards had gripped his arms tightly.

"Well, that didn't work," said Quandrasi.

Lagorna held out her hands again, and Quandrasi handed her the staff, muttering curses under his breath. "Now what?" she asked.

"Destroy it," said Vergil.

"I'll do it," said a booming voice from the square behind them. Yurgi, covered with plaster dust and blood, was hobbling toward them.

"Don't," Quandrasi pleaded. "It's my creation. Everything I worked for!"

Vergil handed Yurgi the staff. She set it on the ground and unceremoniously stomped on the silver globe. Then she picked up the staff and broke it in two, doubled the pieces, broke those as well, and then did it one more time. She handed the pieces back to Quandrasi, who accepted them with a dejected look on his face.

"Watch out!" someone screamed. Looking up at the golem, Vergil saw that its hands had fallen to its side, and its head drooped. The golem swayed back and then forward.

"Get out of the way!" cried Vergil. "It's going to fall!"

The goblins scattered, and Yurgi hobbled out of the way. But Quandrasi continued to stare morosely at the splinters in his hands. "All my work," he murmured.

"You'll find another purpose," said Vergil, glancing up at the golem, which was definitely leaning their direction. "Something productive. Gardening, maybe."

"No," said Quandrasi. "This... this was all I had."

"It doesn't have to be!" cried Vergil. "Just come with me. Please!" He gripped Quandrasi by the arm, but the man made no sign of moving, and Vergil simply didn't have the strength to move the man against his will. A shadow swept over them as the golem fell, and Vergil released the illusionist. He dashed out of the way as the colossus fell, and was thrown to the ground by the concussion under his feet. A cloud of dust erupted around him, and Vergil quickly covered his face with his shirt to avoid breathing in the stuff. He crawled away from the scene, his eyes closed, until a huge hand gripped him by the arm, helping him to his feet. Yurgi.

As the dust began to settle, Vergil and Yurgi strained to see what was left of the golem. Not much, it turned out. The statue was unrecognizable, just piles of rubble strewn across the square. It was as if the hatred that had animated it had also torn it apart. Somewhere under all that mess was the crushed body of Quandrasi. Maybe it was for the best that he hadn't survived. Vergil would like to believe in the possibility of redemption—after all, his own views on goblins had undergone a significant change over the past few days—but it was hard to see how a man driven purely by the desire for destruction could ever become a productive member of society. In any case, the matter was settled: the hatred and malicious delusions of Quandrasi would plague Dis no longer.

Twenty

Cleaning up the debris of *Unity* took over a week. After the mass confusion and terror of Quandrasi's assembly, unrest in the city subsided significantly, mostly because nobody was quite sure anymore who they were supposed to be angry at, or about what.

Marko had been rushed to a doctor shortly after the golem fell, and he received the possible medical treatment. Unfortunately, despite the recent advances in medicine due to the adoption of zelaznium-based technology, the field of microbiology was still in its infancy, and a rampant infection required Marko's leg to be amputated below the knee. Handri offered this development as proof that germs were real, but Vergil pointed out that the application of potions to "kill the germs" hadn't worked, suggesting that evil spirits were the more likely candidate. The matter was never decisively settled.

Yurgi and Handri recovered fully from their injuries, and each returned to service for their respected bosses. Marko, for his part, was just happy to be alive. Chagrined that he owed his life to Vergil, Marko offered to restore to Vergil what he had cheated him out of. Vergil insisted this wasn't necessary; all he really wanted was to live the remainder of his life in peace on his estate. Marko assured him that he would see to the repairs on Vergil's estate as soon as possible.

Vergil, whose fame had been spreading rapidly even before the assembly, was widely considered the hero of the day, and many urged him to run for office now that Thameril had fled the city and Grimble had been found to be an impostor. But Vergil declined, insisting that he had had quite enough excitement. It was time for him to transition gracefully into old age and try to enjoy whatever time he had left. Besides, he argued, Lagorna had been the true hero; it was her rallying of the goblins that had led to the Quandrasi's unmasking and the destruction of the golem. With Vergil's endorsement, Lagorna ran for the open seat in a special election, and won handily. Her first act as the new mayor was to release the prisoners who had been thrown into the dungeons on trumped up charges by CAGE. She then got the council to set up a quasi-governmental body called the Human-Monster Organization for Reconciliation. The purpose of HuMOR was to try to put the antagonism between humans and goblins in the past. The results of HuMOR's efforts were mixed, but you can't please everybody.[4]

Marko met with the council several times to talk about the problem of goblin unemployment, which was the root cause of much of the discord. With Vergil's blessing, he offered to rebuild the Goblintex mill, updating the construction to make it safer and more humane for the workers. The project was approved, and several dozen goblins were hired to build the new mill.

Marko also hired several goblins to work on the repairs to Vergil's estate. Vergil and Handri stayed at Marko's apartment until Vergil's estate was livable, then moved back in. The goblin workers had resided there as well, and Vergil made room for them in the estate while they finished the repairs. Many of them stayed on after the construction was finished, helping Vergil and Marko with gardening and other projects in exchange for room and board. The house was often crowded, but Virgil enjoyed the company.

Vergil lived for another twelve years after the fall of the golem, doing his best to avoid politics and rarely venturing into town. He spent most of his days sitting outside in the sunshine, reading. Sometimes he read old books about the land of Dis of his youth or about the Battle of Brandsveid, but more often he would read about the wonders of zelaznium and the technological advances it had made possible. There was plenty to read on the subject; every week

---

[4] Some argued that the organization should have been called the Human-Monster Organization for *Urban* Reconciliation, but such proposals were rejected by those of sounder mind.

he would send Handri into Avaress on his bicycle for another satchel-ful of books. At least once a month a brand new book would appear detailing some wondrous new invention that somebody had dreamed up, and Vergil would devour the book in one sitting. He didn't know what the end result of all these changes would be, and he doubted he would live to see the final result, but he knew that Dis would never again be the land he remembered from before his slumber.

It was, by and large, a happy existence. Only one thing occasionally bothered him, usually on rainy days when he was forced to sit inside, where he had trouble reading with his failing eyes. His thoughts would drift to the day that the golem fell, smashing into a million pieces, and how he had been unable to save Quandrasi from his own destruction. What bothered him wasn't so much the idea of Quandrasi being crushed but the fact that he hadn't actually *seen* Quandrasi crushed. It was certainly possible that Quandrasi had been as disheartened as he had appeared, but Quandrasi was also an exceptionally talented actor and illusionist. Had he faked his own death to escape justice for his crimes? As far as Vergil knew, no body had ever been found, but that meant little. The cleanup efforts had been chaotic and largely unsupervised, and by the time Vergil had thought to ask to be informed when Quandrasi's body was found, the remnants of the statue and much of the broken pavement had already been carted off. Vergil assured himself that escape would have been impossible; Vergil had avoided being crushed by mere inches.

And yet... if anybody could have escaped, it would be Quandrasi. Vergil kept his suspicion to himself; there was no point in fanning the flames of fear in Avaressa. But many times before Vergil died, he found himself wondering if hate might someday rise again to threaten the civilization of Dis.

Review this book!
Did you enjoy *Disillusioned?* Please take a moment to leave a review on your favorite book reviewing website! Reviews are very important for getting the word out to other readers, and it only takes a few seconds.

More books in the Dis series:
    Disenchanted
    Distopia

More books by Robert Kroese you might enjoy:
    Mercury Falls
    Mercury Rises
    Mercury Rests
    Mercury Revolts
    "Mercury Begins" (short story)
    "The Chicolini Incident" (short story)
    Starship Grifters
    Schrödinger's Gat
    City of Sand
    The Foreworld Saga: The Outcast
    The Force is Middling in This One

Made in the USA
Middletown, DE
09 August 2018